Feature Engineering for Machine Learning
Principles and Techniques for Data Scientists

Alice Zheng and Amanda Casari

Beijing · Boston · Farnham · Sebastopol · Tokyo

Feature Engineering for Machine Learning

by Alice Zheng and Amanda Casari

Published by O'Reilly Media, Inc., 1005 Gravenstein Highway North, Sebastopol, CA 95472.

O'Reilly books may be purchased for educational, business, or sales promotional use. Online editions are also available for most titles (*http://oreilly.com/safari*). For more information, contact our corporate/institutional sales department: 800-998-9938 or *corporate@oreilly.com*.

Editors: Rachel Roumeliotis and Jeff Bleiel
Production Editor: Kristen Brown
Copyeditor: Rachel Head
Proofreader: Sonia Saruba

Indexer: Ellen Troutman
Interior Designer: David Futato
Cover Designer: Karen Montgomery
Illustrator: Rebecca Demarest

April 2018:   First Edition

Revision History for the First Edition
2018-03-23:   First Release

See *http://oreilly.com/catalog/errata.csp?isbn=9781491953242* for release details.

978-1-491-95324-2

[LSI]

Table of Contents

Preface

Introduction

Machine learning fits mathematical models to data in order to derive insights or make predictions. These models take features as input. A *feature* is a numeric representation of an aspect of raw data. Features sit between data and models in the machine learning pipeline. *Feature engineering* is the act of extracting features from raw data and transforming them into formats that are suitable for the machine learning model. It is a crucial step in the machine learning pipeline, because the right features can ease the difficulty of modeling, and therefore enable the pipeline to output results of higher quality. Practitioners agree that the vast majority of time in building a machine learning pipeline is spent on feature engineering and data cleaning. Yet, despite its importance, the topic is rarely discussed on its own. Perhaps this is because the right features can only be defined in the context of both the model and the data; since data and models are so diverse, it's difficult to generalize the practice of feature engineering across projects.

Nevertheless, feature engineering is not just an ad hoc practice. There are deeper principles at work, and they are best illustrated in situ. Each chapter of this book addresses one data problem: how to represent text data or image data, how to reduce the dimensionality of autogenerated features, when and how to normalize, etc. Think of this as a collection of interconnected short stories, as opposed to a single long novel. Each chapter provides a vignette into the vast array of existing feature engineering techniques. Together, they illustrate the overarching principles.

Mastering a subject is not just about knowing the definitions and being able to derive the formulas. It is not enough to know how the mechanism works and what it can do —one must also understand why it is designed that way, how it relates to other techniques, and what the pros and cons of each approach are. Mastery is about knowing precisely how something is done, having an intuition for the underlying principles, and integrating it into one's existing web of knowledge. One does not become a master of something by simply reading a book, though a good book can open new doors.

It has to involve practice—putting the ideas to use, which is an iterative process. With every iteration, we know the ideas better and become increasingly more adept and creative at applying them. The goal of this book is to facilitate the application of its ideas.

This book tries to teach the reason first, and the mathematics second. Instead of only discussing *how* something is done, we try to teach *why*. Our goal is to provide the *intuition* behind the ideas, so that the reader may understand how and when to apply them. There are tons of descriptions and pictures for folks who learn in different ways. Mathematical formulas are presented in order to make the intuition precise, and also to bridge this book with other existing offerings.

Code examples in this book are given in Python, using a variety of free and open source packages. The NumPy (*http://www.numpy.org/*) library provides numeric vector and matrix operations. Pandas (*http://pandas.pydata.org/*) provides the Data-Frame that is the building block of data science in Python. Scikit-learn (*http://scikit-learn.org/stable/*) is a general-purpose machine learning package with extensive coverage of models and feature transformers. Matplotlib (*https://matplotlib.org/*) and the styling library Seaborn (*https://seaborn.pydata.org/*) provide plotting and visualization support. You can find these examples as Jupyter notebooks in our GitHub repo (*https://github.com/alicezheng/feature-engineering-book*).

The first few chapters start out slow in order to provide a bridge for folks who are just getting started with data science and machine learning. Chapter 1 introduces the fundamental concepts in the machine learning pipeline (data, models, features, etc.). In Chapter 2, we explore basic feature engineering for numeric data: filtering, binning, scaling, log transforms and power transforms, and interaction features. Chapter 3 dives into feature engineering for natural text, exploring techniques like bag-of-words, *n*-grams, and phrase detection. Chapter 4 examines tf-idf (term frequency-inverse document frequency) as an example of feature scaling and discusses why it works. The pace starts to pick up around Chapter 5, where we talk about efficient encoding techniques for categorical variables, including feature hashing and bin counting. By the time we get to principal component analysis (PCA) in Chapter 6, we are deep in the land of machine learning. Chapter 7 looks at *k*-means as a featurization technique, which illustrates the useful concept of model stacking. Chapter 8 is all about images, which are much more challenging in terms of feature extraction than text data. We look at two manual feature extraction techniques, SIFT and HOG, before concluding with an explanation of deep learning as the latest feature extraction technique for images. We finish up in Chapter 9 by showing a few different techniques in an end-to-end example, creating a recommender for a dataset of academic papers.

In Living Color

The illustrations in this book are best viewed in color. Really, you should print out the color versions of the Swiss roll in Chapter 7 and paste them into your book. Your aesthetic sense will thank us.

Feature engineering is a vast topic, and more methods are being invented every day, particularly in the area of automatic feature learning. In order to limit the book to a manageable size, we've had to make some cuts. This book does not discuss Fourier analysis for audio data, though it is a beautiful subject that is closely related to eigen analysis in linear algebra (which we touch upon in Chapters 4 and 6). We also skip a discussion of random features, which are intimately related to Fourier analysis. We provide an introduction to feature learning via deep learning for image data, but do not go into depth on the numerous deep learning models under active development. Also out of scope are advanced research ideas like random projections, complex text featurization models such as word2vec and Brown clustering, and latent space models like Latent Dirichlet allocation and matrix factorization. If those words mean nothing to you, then you are in luck. If the frontiers of feature learning are where your interest lies, then this is probably not the book for you.

The book assumes knowledge of basic machine learning concepts, such as what a model is and what a vector is, though a refresher is provided so we're all on the same page. Experience with linear algebra, probability distributions, and optimization are helpful, but not necessary.

Conventions Used in This Book

The following typographical conventions are used in this book:

Italic
> Indicates new terms, URLs, email addresses, filenames, and file extensions.

`Constant width`
> Used for program listings, as well as within paragraphs to refer to program elements such as variable or function names, databases, data types, environment variables, statements, and keywords.

`Constant width bold`
> Shows commands or other text that should be typed literally by the user.

`Constant width italic`
> Shows text that should be replaced with user-supplied values or by values determined by context.

The book also contains numerous linear algebra equations. We use the following conventions with regard to notation: scalars are shown in lowercase italic (e.g., a), vectors in lowercase bold (e.g., $\mathbf{v}$), and matrices in uppercase bold and italic (e.g., $\boldsymbol{U}$).

This element signifies a tip or suggestion.

This element signifies a general note.

This element indicates a warning or caution.

Using Code Examples

Supplemental material (code examples, exercises, etc.) is available for download at *https://github.com/alicezheng/feature-engineering-book*.

This book is here to help you get your job done. In general, if example code is offered with this book, you may use it in your programs and documentation. You do not need to contact us for permission unless you're reproducing a significant portion of the code. For example, writing a program that uses several chunks of code from this book does not require permission. Selling or distributing a CD-ROM of examples from O'Reilly books does require permission. Answering a question by citing this book and quoting example code does not require permission. Incorporating a significant amount of example code from this book into your product's documentation does require permission.

We appreciate, but do not require, attribution. An attribution usually includes the title, author, publisher, and ISBN. For example: "*Feature Engineering for Machine Learning* by Alice Zheng and Amanda Casari (O'Reilly). Copyright 2018 Alice Zheng and Amanda Casari, 978-1-491-95324-2."

If you feel your use of code examples falls outside fair use or the permission given above, feel free to contact us at *permissions@oreilly.com*.

O'Reilly Safari

 *Safari* (formerly Safari Books Online) is a membership-based training and reference platform for enterprise, government, educators, and individuals.

Members have access to thousands of books, training videos, Learning Paths, interactive tutorials, and curated playlists from over 250 publishers, including O'Reilly Media, Harvard Business Review, Prentice Hall Professional, Addison-Wesley Professional, Microsoft Press, Sams, Que, Peachpit Press, Adobe, Focal Press, Cisco Press, John Wiley & Sons, Syngress, Morgan Kaufmann, IBM Redbooks, Packt, Adobe Press, FT Press, Apress, Manning, New Riders, McGraw-Hill, Jones & Bartlett, and Course Technology, among others.

For more information, please visit *http://oreilly.com/safari*.

How to Contact Us

Please address comments and questions concerning this book to the publisher:

> O'Reilly Media, Inc.
> 1005 Gravenstein Highway North
> Sebastopol, CA 95472
> 800-998-9938 (in the United States or Canada)
> 707-829-0515 (international or local)
> 707-829-0104 (fax)

We have a web page for this book, where we list errata, examples, and any additional information. You can access this page at *http://bit.ly/featureEngineering_for_ML*.

To comment or ask technical questions about this book, send email to *bookquestions@oreilly.com*.

For more information about our books, courses, conferences, and news, see our website at *http://www.oreilly.com*.

Find us on Facebook: *http://facebook.com/oreilly*

Follow us on Twitter: *http://twitter.com/oreillymedia*

Watch us on YouTube: *http://www.youtube.com/oreillymedia*

Acknowledgments

First and foremost, we want to thank our editors, Shannon Cutt and Jeff Bleiel, for shepherding two first-time authors through the (unknown to us) long marathon of book publishing. Without your many check-ins, this book would not have seen the light of day. Thank you also to Ben Lorica, O'Reilly Mastermind, whose encouragement and affirmation turned this from a crazy idea into an actual product. Thank you to Kristen Brown and the O'Reilly production team for their superb attention to detail and extreme patience in waiting for our responses.

If it takes a village to raise a child, it takes a parliament of data scientists to publish a book. We greatly appreciate every hashtag suggestion, notes on room for improvement and calls for clarification. Andreas Müller, Sethu Raman, and Antoine Atallah took precious time out of their busy days to provide technical reviews. Antoine not only did so at lightning speed, but also made available his beefy machines for use on experiments. Ted Dunning's statistical fluency and mastery of applied machine learning are legendary. He is also incredibly generous with his time and his ideas, and he literally gave us the method and the example described in the k-means chapter. Owen Zhang revealed his cache of Kaggle nuggets on using response rate features, which were added to machine learning folklore on bin-counting collected by Misha Bilenko. Thank you also to Alex Ott, Francisco Martin, and David Garrison for additional feedback.

Special Thanks from Alice

I would like to thank the GraphLab/Dato/Turi family for their generous support in the first phase of this project. The idea germinated from interactions with our users. In the process of building a brand new machine learning platform for data scientists, we discovered that the world needs a more systematic understanding of feature engineering. Thank you to Carlos Guestrin for granting me leave from busy startup life to focus on writing.

Thank you to Amanda, who started out as technical reviewer and later pitched in to help bring this book to life. You are the best finisher! Now that this book is done, we'll have to find another project, if only to keep doing our editing sessions over tea and coffee and sandwiches and takeout food.

Special thanks to my friend and healer, Daisy Thompson, for her unwavering support throughout all phases of this project. Without your help, I would have taken much longer to take the plunge, and would have resented the marathon. You brought light and relief to this project, as you do with all your work.

Special Thanks from Amanda

As this is a book and not a lifetime achievement award, I will attempt to scope my thanks to the project at hand.

Many thanks to Alice for bringing me in as a technical editor and then coauthor. I continue to learn so much from you, including how to write better math jokes and explain complex concepts clearly.

Last in order only, special thanks to my husband, Matthew, for mastering the nearly impossible role of grounding me, encouraging me towards my next goal, and never allowing a concept to be hand-waved away. You are the best partner and my favorite partner in crime. To the biggest and littlest sunshines, you inspire me to make you proud.

## CHAPTER 1

The Machine Learning Pipeline

Before diving into feature engineering, let's take a moment to take a look at the over-all machine learning pipeline. This will help us get situated in the larger picture of the application. To that end, we'll begin with a little musing on the basic concepts like *data* and *models*.

Data

What we call *data* are observations of real-world phenomena. For instance, stock market data might involve observations of daily stock prices, announcements of earnings by individual companies, and even opinion articles from pundits. Personal biometric data can include measurements of our minute-by-minute heart rate, blood sugar level, blood pressure, etc. Customer intelligence data includes observations such as "Alice bought two books on Sunday," "Bob browsed these pages on the web-site," and "Charlie clicked on the special offer link from last week." We can come up with endless examples of data across different domains.

Each piece of data provides a small window into a limited aspect of reality. The col-lection of all of these observations gives us a picture of the whole. But the picture is messy because it is composed of a thousand little pieces, and there's always measure-ment noise and missing pieces.

Tasks

Why do we collect data? There are questions that data can help us answer—questions like "Which stocks I should invest in?" or "How can I live a healthier lifestyle?" or "How can I understand my customers' changing tastes, so that my business can serve them better?"

The path from data to answers is full of false starts and dead ends (see Figure 1-1). What starts out as a promising approach may not pan out. What was originally just a hunch may end up leading to the best solution. Workflows with data are frequently multistage, iterative processes. For instance, stock prices are observed at the exchange, aggregated by an intermediary like Thomson Reuters, stored in a database, bought by a company, converted into a Hive store on a Hadoop cluster, pulled out of the store by a script, subsampled, massaged, and cleaned by another script, dumped to a file, and converted to a format that you can try out in your favorite modeling library in R, Python, or Scala. The predictions are then dumped back out to a CSV file and parsed by an evaluator, and the model is iterated multiple times, rewritten in C++ or Java by your production team, and run on all of the data before the final predictions are pumped out to another database.

Figure 1-1. The garden of bifurcating paths between data and answers

However, if we disregard the mess of tools and systems for a moment, we might see that the process involves two mathematical entities that are the bread and butter of machine learning: *models* and *features*.

Models

Trying to understand the world through data is like trying to piece together reality using a noisy, incomplete jigsaw puzzle with a bunch of extra pieces. This is where mathematical modeling—in particular statistical modeling—comes in. The language of statistics contains concepts for many frequent characteristics of data, such as *wrong*, *redundant*, or *missing*. Wrong data is the result of a mistake in measurement. Redundant data contains multiple aspects that convey exactly the same information. For instance, the day of week may be present as a categorical variable with values of "Monday," "Tuesday," … "Sunday," and again included as an integer value between 0 and 6. If this day-of-week information is not present for some data points, then you've got missing data on your hands.

A *mathematical model* of data describes the relationships between different aspects of the data. For instance, a model that predicts stock prices might be a formula that maps a company's earning history, past stock prices, and industry to the predicted stock price. A model that recommends music might measure the similarity between users (based on their listening habits), and recommend the same artists to users who have listened to a lot of the same songs.

Mathematical formulas relate numeric quantities to each other. But raw data is often not numeric. (The action "Alice bought *The Lord of the Rings* trilogy on Wednesday" is not numeric, and neither is the review that she subsequently writes about the book.) There must be a piece that connects the two together. This is where features come in.

Features

A *feature* is a numeric representation of raw data. There are many ways to turn raw data into numeric measurements, which is why features can end up looking like a lot of things. Naturally, features must derive from the type of data that is available. Perhaps less obvious is the fact that they are also tied to the model; some models are more appropriate for some types of features, and vice versa. The right features are relevant to the task at hand and should be easy for the model to ingest. *Feature engineering* is the process of formulating the most appropriate features given the data, the model, and the task.

The number of features is also important. If there are not enough informative features, then the model will be unable to perform the ultimate task. If there are too many features, or if most of them are irrelevant, then the model will be more expensive and tricky to train. Something might go awry in the training process that impacts the model's performance.

Model Evaluation

Features and models sit between raw data and the desired insights (see Figure 1-2). In a machine learning workflow, we pick not only the model, but also the features. This is a double-jointed lever, and the choice of one affects the other. Good features make the subsequent modeling step easy and the resulting model more capable of completing the desired task. Bad features may require a much more complicated model to achieve the same level of performance. In the rest of this book, we will cover different kinds of features and discuss their pros and cons for different types of data and models. Without further ado, let's get started!

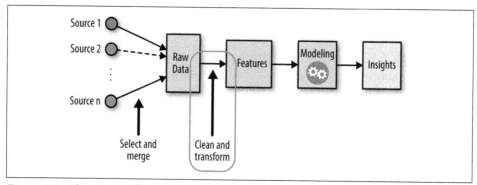

Figure 1-2. The place of feature engineering in the machine learning workflow

## CHAPTER 2

Fancy Tricks with Simple Numbers

Before diving into complex data types such as text and image, let's start with the simplest: numeric data. This may come from a variety of sources: geolocation of a place or a person, the price of a purchase, measurements from a sensor, traffic counts, etc. Numeric data is already in a format that's easily ingestible by mathematical models. This doesn't mean that feature engineering is no longer necessary, though. Good features should not only represent salient aspects of the data, but also conform to the assumptions of the model. Hence, transformations are often necessary. Numeric feature engineering techniques are fundamental. They can be applied whenever raw data is converted into numeric features.

The first sanity check for numeric data is whether the magnitude matters. Do we just need to know whether it's positive or negative? Or perhaps we only need to know the magnitude at a very coarse granularity? This sanity check is particularly important for automatically accrued numbers such as counts—the number of daily visits to a website, the number of reviews garnered by a restaurant, etc.

Next, consider the scale of the features. What are the largest and the smallest values? Do they span several orders of magnitude? Models that are smooth functions of input features are sensitive to the scale of the input. For example, $3x + 1$ is a simple linear function of the input x, and the scale of its output depends directly on the scale of the input. Other examples include k-means clustering, nearest neighbors methods, radial basis function (RBF) kernels, and anything that uses the Euclidean distance. For these models and modeling components, it is often a good idea to *normalize* the features so that the output stays on an expected scale.

Logical functions, on the other hand, are not sensitive to input feature scale. Their output is binary no matter what the inputs are. For instance, the logical AND takes any two variables and outputs 1 if and only if both of the inputs are true. Another example of a logical function is the step function (e.g., is input x greater than 5?).

Decision tree models consist of step functions of input features. Hence, models based on space-partitioning trees (decision trees, gradient boosted machines, random forests) are not sensitive to scale. The only exception is if the scale of the input grows over time, which is the case if the feature is an accumulated count of some sort—eventually it will grow outside of the range that the tree was trained on. If this might be the case, then it might be necessary to rescale the inputs periodically. Another solution is the bin-counting method discussed in Chapter 5.

It's also important to consider the distribution of numeric features. Distribution summarizes the probability of taking on a particular value. The distribution of input features matters to some models more than others. For instance, the training process of a linear regression model assumes that prediction errors are distributed like a Gaussian (*http://mathworld.wolfram.com/NormalDistribution.html*). This is usually fine, except when the prediction target spreads out over several orders of magnitude. In this case, the Gaussian error assumption likely no longer holds. One way to deal with this is to transform the output target in order to tame the magnitude of the growth. (Strictly speaking this would be target engineering, not feature engineering.) Log transforms, which are a type of *power transform*, take the distribution of the variable closer to Gaussian.

In addition to features tailoring to the assumptions of the model or training process, multiple features can be composed together into more complex features. The hope is that complex features can more succinctly capture important information in raw data. Making the input features more "eloquent" allows the model itself to be simpler, easier to train and evaluate, and to make better predictions. Taken to an extreme, complex features may themselves be the output of statistical models. This is a concept known as *model stacking*, which we discuss in much more detail in Chapters 7 and 8. In this chapter, we give the simplest example of complex features: *interaction features*.

Interaction features are simple to formulate, but the combination of features results in many more being input into the model. In order to reduce the computational expense, it is usually necessary to prune the input features using automatic *feature selection*.

We'll begin with the basic concepts of scalars, vectors, and spaces, followed by discussions of scale, distribution, interaction features, and feature selection.

Scalars, Vectors, and Spaces

Before we go any further, we need to define some basic concepts that underlie the rest of this book. A single numeric feature is also known as a *scalar*. An ordered list of scalars is known as a *vector*. Vectors sit within a *vector space*. In the vast majority of machine learning applications, the input to a model is usually represented as a numeric vector. The rest of this book will discuss best-practice strategies for converting raw data into a vector of numbers.

A vector can be visualized as a point in space. (Sometimes people draw a line or arrow from the origin to that point. In this book, we will mostly use just the point.) For instance, suppose we have a two-dimensional vector $\mathbf{v} = [1, -1]$. The vector contains two numbers: in the first direction, d_1, the vector has a value of 1, and in the second direction, d_2, it has a value of -1. We can plot $\mathbf{v}$ in a 2D plot, as shown in Figure 2-1.

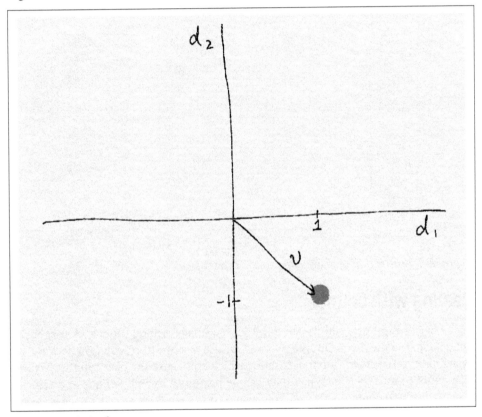

Figure 2-1. A single vector

In the world of data, an abstract vector and its feature dimensions take on actual meaning. For instance, a vector can represent a person's preference for songs. Each song is a feature, where a value of 1 is equivalent to a thumbs-up, and -1 a thumbs-down. Suppose the vector $\mathbf{v}$ represents the preferences of a listener, Bob. Bob likes "Blowin' in the Wind" by Bob Dylan and "Poker Face" by Lady Gaga. Other people might have different preferences. Collectively, a collection of data can be visualized in *feature space* as a point cloud.

Conversely, a song can be represented by the individual preferences of a group of people. Suppose there are only two listeners, Alice and Bob. Alice likes "Poker Face," "Blowin' in the Wind," and "Hallelujah" by Leonard Cohen, but hates Katy Perry's "Roar" and Radiohead's "Creep." Bob likes "Roar," "Hallelujah," and "Blowin' in the Wind," but hates "Poker Face" and "Creep." Each song is a point in the space of listeners. Just like we can visualize data in feature space, we can visualize features in *data space*. Figure 2-2 shows this example.

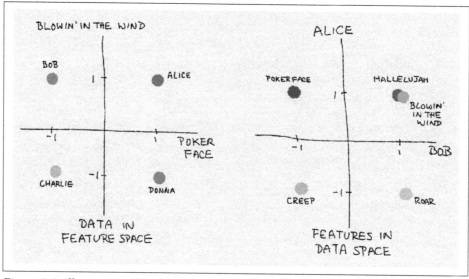

Figure 2-2. Illustration of feature space versus data space

Dealing with Counts

In the age of Big Data, counts can quickly accumulate without bound. A user might put a song or a movie on infinite playback or use a script to repeatedly check for the availability of tickets for a popular show, which will cause the play count or website visit count to quickly rise. When data can be produced at high volume and velocity, it's very likely to contain a few extreme values. It is a good idea to check the scale and determine whether to keep the data as raw numbers, convert them into binary values to indicate presence, or bin them into coarser granularity. To illustrate these ideas, let's look at a few examples.

Binarization

The Echo Nest Taste Profile subset (*http://labrosa.ee.columbia.edu/millionsong/taste profile*), the official user data collection for the Million Song Dataset, contains the full music listening histories of one million users on Echo Nest. Here are some relevant statistics about the dataset:

Statistics on the Echo Nest Taste Profile Dataset

- There are more than 48 million triplets of user ID, song ID, and listen count.
- The full dataset contains 1,019,318 unique users and 384,546 unique songs.

Suppose our task is to build a recommender to recommend songs to users. One component of the recommender might predict how much a user will enjoy a particular song. Since the data contains actual listen counts, should that be the target of the prediction? This would be the right thing to do if a large listen count means the user really likes the song and a low listen count means they're not interested in it. However, the data shows that while 99% of the listen counts are 24 or lower, there are also some listen counts in the thousands, with the maximum being 9,667. (As Figure 2-3 shows, the histogram peaks in the bin closest to 0. But more than 10,000 triplets have greater counts, with a few in the thousands.) These values are anomalously large; if we were to try to predict the actual listen counts, the model would be pulled off course by these large values.

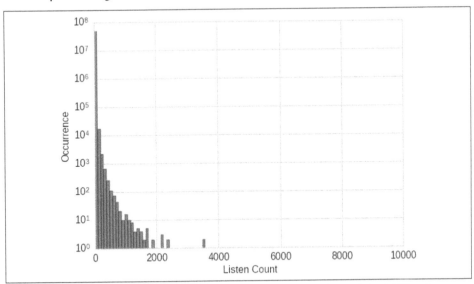

Figure 2-3. Histogram of listen counts in the Taste Profile subset of the Million Song Dataset (http://labrosa.ee.columbia.edu/millionsong/)—note that the y-axis is on a log scale

In the Million Song Dataset, the raw listen count is not a *robust* measure of user taste. (In statistical lingo, robustness means that the method works under a wide variety of conditions.) Users have different listening habits. Some people might put their favorite songs on infinite loop, while others might savor them only on special occasions. We can't necessarily say that someone who listens to a song 20 times must like it twice as much as someone else who listens to it 10 times.

A more robust representation of user preference is to binarize the count and clip all counts greater than 1 to 1, as illustrated in Example 2-1. In other words, if the user listened to a song at least once, then we count it as the user liking the song. This way, the model will not need to spend cycles on predicting the minute differences between the raw counts. The binary target is a simple and robust measure of user preference.

Example 2-1. Binarizing listen counts in the Million Song Dataset

```
>>> import pandas as pd
>>> listen_count = pd.read_csv('millionsong/train_triplets.txt.zip',
...                            header=None, delimiter='\t')
# The table contains user-song-count triplets. Only nonzero counts are
# included. Hence, to binarize the count, we just need to set the entire
# count column to 1.
>>> listen_count[2] = 1
```

This is an example where we engineer the target variable of the model. Strictly speaking, the target is not a feature because it's not the input. But on occasion we do need to modify the target in order to solve the right problem.

Quantization or Binning

For this exercise, we take data from round 6 of the Yelp dataset challenge (*http://www.yelp.com/dataset_challenge*) and create a much smaller classification dataset. The Yelp dataset contains user reviews of businesses from 10 cities across North America and Europe. Each business is labeled with zero or more categories.

Statistics on the Yelp Reviews Dataset (Round 6)

- There are 782 business categories.
- The full dataset contains 1,569,264 ($\approx$1.6M) reviews and 61,184 (61K) businesses.
- "Restaurants" (990,627 reviews) and "Nightlife" (210,028 reviews) are the most popular categories, review count–wise.
- No business is categorized as both a restaurant and a nightlife venue. So, there is no overlap between the two groups of reviews.

Each business has a review count. Suppose our task is to use collaborative filtering to predict the rating a user might give to a business. The review count might be a useful input feature because there is usually a strong correlation between popularity and good ratings. Now the question is, should we use the raw review count or process it further? Figure 2-4, produced by Example 2-2, shows the histogram of all business review counts. We see the same pattern as in the listen counts in the previous example: most of the counts are small, but some businesses have reviews in the thousands.

Example 2-2. Visualizing business review counts in the Yelp dataset

```
>>> import pandas as pd
>>> import json

# Load the data about businesses
>>> biz_file = open('yelp_academic_dataset_business.json')
>>> biz_df = pd.DataFrame([json.loads(x) for x in biz_file.readlines()])
>>> biz_file.close()

>>> import matplotlib.pyplot as plt
>>> import seaborn as sns

# Plot the histogram of the review counts
>>> sns.set_style('whitegrid')
>>> fig, ax = plt.subplots()
>>> biz_df['review_count'].hist(ax=ax, bins=100)
>>> ax.set_yscale('log')
>>> ax.tick_params(labelsize=14)
>>> ax.set_xlabel('Review Count', fontsize=14)
>>> ax.set_ylabel('Occurrence', fontsize=14)
```

Raw counts that span several orders of magnitude are problematic for many models. In a linear model, the same linear coefficient would have to work for all possible values of the count. Large counts could also wreak havoc in unsupervised learning methods such as *k*-means clustering, which uses Euclidean distance as a similarity function to measure the similarity between data points. A large count in one element of the data vector would outweigh the similarity in all other elements, which could throw off the entire similarity measurement.

One solution is to contain the scale by *quantizing* the count. In other words, we group the counts into bins, and get rid of the actual count values. Quantization maps a continuous number to a discrete one. We can think of the discretized numbers as an ordered sequence of bins that represent a measure of intensity.

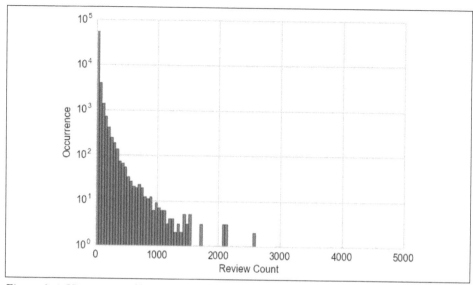

Figure 2-4. Histogram of business review counts in the Yelp reviews dataset—the y-axis is on a log scale

In order to quantize data, we have to decide how wide each bin should be. The solutions fall into two categories: fixed-width or adaptive. We will give an example of each type.

Fixed-width binning

With fixed-width binning, each bin contains a specific numeric range. The ranges can be custom designed or automatically segmented, and they can be linearly scaled or exponentially scaled. For example, we can group people into age ranges by decade: 0–9 years old in bin 1, 10–19 years in bin 2, etc. To map from the count to the bin, we simply divide by the width of the bin and take the integer part.

It's also common to see custom-designed age ranges that better correspond to stages of life, such as:

- 0–12 years old
- 12–17 years old
- 18–24 years old
- 25–34 years old
- 35–44 years old
- 45–54 years old
- 55–64 years old

- 65–74 years old

- 75 years or older

When the numbers span multiple magnitudes, it may be better to group by powers of 10 (or powers of any constant): 0–9, 10–99, 100–999, 1000–9999, etc. The bin widths grow exponentially, going from $O(10)$, to $O(100)$, $O(1000)$, and beyond. To map from the count to the bin, we take the log of the count. Exponential-width binning is very much related to the log transform, which we discuss in "Log Transformation" on page 15. Example 2-3 illustrates several of these binning methods.

Example 2-3. Quantizing counts with fixed-width bins

```
>>> import numpy as np

# Generate 20 random integers uniformly between 0 and 99
>>> small_counts = np.random.randint(0, 100, 20)
>>> small_counts
array([30, 64, 49, 26, 69, 23, 56,  7, 69, 67, 87, 14, 67, 33, 88, 77, 75,
       47, 44, 93])
# Map to evenly spaced bins 0-9 by division
>>> np.floor_divide(small_counts, 10)
array([3, 6, 4, 2, 6, 2, 5, 0, 6, 6, 8, 1, 6, 3, 8, 7, 7, 4, 4, 9], dtype=int32)

# An array of counts that span several magnitudes
>>> large_counts = [296, 8286, 64011, 80, 3, 725, 867, 2215, 7689, 11495, 91897,
...                 44, 28, 7971, 926, 122, 22222]
# Map to exponential-width bins via the log function
>>> np.floor(np.log10(large_counts))
array([ 2.,  3.,  4.,  1.,  0.,  2.,  2.,  3.,  3.,  4.,  4.,  1.,  1.,
        3.,  2.,  2.,  4.])
```

Quantile binning

Fixed-width binning is easy to compute. But if there are large gaps in the counts, then there will be many empty bins with no data. This problem can be solved by adaptively positioning the bins based on the distribution of the data. This can be done using the quantiles of the distribution.

Quantiles are values that divide the data into equal portions. For example, the median divides the data in halves; half the data points are smaller and half larger than the median. The quartiles divide the data into quarters, the deciles into tenths, etc. Example 2-4 demonstrates how to compute the deciles of the Yelp business review counts, and Figure 2-5 overlays the deciles on the histogram. This gives a much clearer picture of the skew toward smaller counts.

Example 2-4. Computing deciles of Yelp business review counts

```
>>> deciles = biz_df['review_count'].quantile([.1, .2, .3, .4, .5, .6, .7, .8, .9])
>>> deciles
0.1     3.0
0.2     4.0
0.3     5.0
0.4     6.0
0.5     8.0
0.6    12.0
0.7    17.0
0.8    28.0
0.9    58.0
Name: review_count, dtype: float64

# Visualize the deciles on the histogram
>>> sns.set_style('whitegrid')
>>> fig, ax = plt.subplots()
>>> biz_df['review_count'].hist(ax=ax, bins=100)
>>> for pos in deciles:
...     handle = plt.axvline(pos, color='r')
>>> ax.legend([handle], ['deciles'], fontsize=14)
>>> ax.set_yscale('log')
>>> ax.set_xscale('log')
>>> ax.tick_params(labelsize=14)
>>> ax.set_xlabel('Review Count', fontsize=14)
>>> ax.set_ylabel('Occurrence', fontsize=14)
```

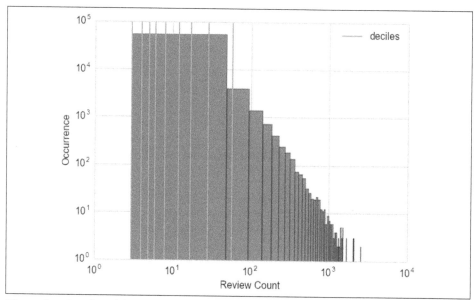

Figure 2-5. Deciles of the review counts in the Yelp reviews dataset—both the x- and y-axes are on a log scale

To compute the quantiles and map data into quantile bins, we can use the Pandas library, as shown in Example 2-5. `pandas.DataFrame.quantile` (*http://bit.ly/2I8vpf2*) and `pandas.Series.quantile` (*http://bit.ly/2D89r80*) compute the quantiles. pan das.qcut (*http://bit.ly/2IamSrY*) maps data into a desired number of quantiles.

Example 2-5. Binning counts by quantiles

```
# Continue example 2-3 with large_counts
>>> import pandas as pd

# Map the counts to quartiles
>>> pd.qcut(large_counts, 4, labels=False)
array([1, 2, 3, 0, 0, 1, 1, 2, 2, 3, 3, 0, 0, 2, 1, 0, 3], dtype=int64)

# Compute the quantiles themselves
>>> large_counts_series = pd.Series(large_counts)
>>> large_counts_series.quantile([0.25, 0.5, 0.75])
0.25     122.0
0.50     926.0
0.75    8286.0
dtype: float64
```

Log Transformation

In the previous section, we briefly introduced the notion of taking the logarithm of the count to map the data to exponential-width bins. Let's take a closer look at that now.

The log function is the inverse of the exponential function. It is defined such that $\log_a(a^x) = x$, where a is a positive constant, and x can be any positive number. Since $a^0 = 1$, we have $\log_a(1) = 0$. This means that the log function maps the small range of numbers between $(0, 1)$ to the entire range of negative numbers $(-\infty, 0)$. The function $\log_{10}(x)$ maps the range of $[1, 10]$ to $[0, 1]$, $[10, 100]$ to $[1, 2]$, and so on. In other words, the log function compresses the range of large numbers and expands the range of small numbers. The larger x is, the slower $\log(x)$ increments.

This is easier to digest by looking at a plot of the log function (see Figure 2-6). Note how the horizontal x values from 100 to 1,000 get compressed into just 2.0 to 3.0 in the vertical y range, while the tiny horizontal portion of x values less than 100 are mapped to the rest of the vertical range.

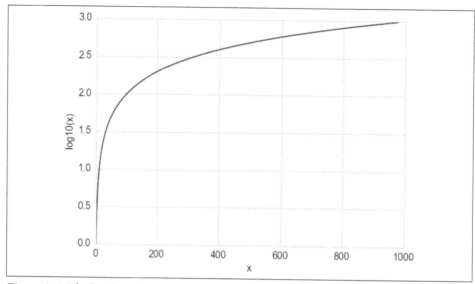

Figure 2-6. The log function compresses the high numeric range and expands the low range

The log transform is a powerful tool for dealing with positive numbers with a heavy-tailed distribution. (A heavy-tailed distribution places more probability mass in the tail range than a Gaussian distribution.) It compresses the long tail in the high end of the distribution into a shorter tail, and expands the low end into a longer head. Figure 2-7 compares the histograms of Yelp business review counts before and after log transformation (see Example 2-6). The y-axes are now both on a normal (linear) scale. The increased bin spacing in the bottom plot between the range of (0.5, 1] is due to there being only 10 possible integer counts between 1 and 10. Notice that the original review counts are very concentrated in the low count region, with outliers stretching out above 4,000. After log transformation, the histogram is less concentrated in the low end and more spread out over the x-axis.

Example 2-6. Visualizing the distribution of review counts before and after log transform

```
>>> fig, (ax1, ax2) = plt.subplots(2,1)
>>> biz_df['review_count'].hist(ax=ax1, bins=100)
>>> ax1.tick_params(labelsize=14)
>>> ax1.set_xlabel('review_count', fontsize=14)
>>> ax1.set_ylabel('Occurrence', fontsize=14)

>>> biz_df['log_review_count'].hist(ax=ax2, bins=100)
>>> ax2.tick_params(labelsize=14)
>>> ax2.set_xlabel('log10(review_count))', fontsize=14)
>>> ax2.set_ylabel('Occurrence', fontsize=14)
```

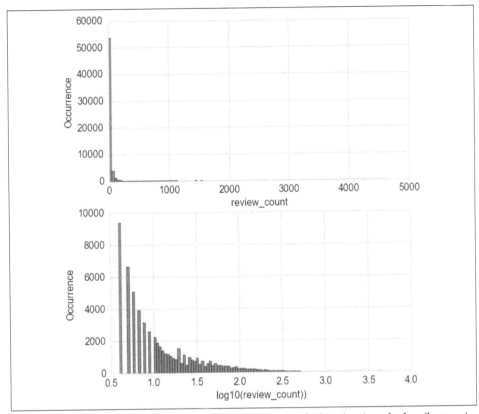

Figure 2-7. Comparison of Yelp business review counts before (top) and after (bottom) log transformation

As another example, let's consider the Online News Popularity dataset (*https:// archive.ics.uci.edu/ml/datasets/Online+News+Popularity*) from the UC Irvine Machine Learning Repository (Fernandes et al., 2015).

Statistics on the Online News Popularity Dataset

- The dataset includes 60 features of a set of 39,797 news articles published by Mashable over a period of 2 years.

Our goal is to use these features to predict the popularity of the articles in terms of the number of shares on social media. In this example, we'll focus on only one feature —the number of words in the article. Figure 2-8 shows the histograms of the feature before and after log transformation (see Example 2-7). Notice that the distribution looks much more Gaussian after log transformation, with the exception of the burst of number of articles of length zero (no content).

Example 2-7. Visualizing the distribution of news article popularity with and without log transformation

```
>>> fig, (ax1, ax2) = plt.subplots(2,1)
>>> df['n_tokens_content'].hist(ax=ax1, bins=100)
>>> ax1.tick_params(labelsize=14)
>>> ax1.set_xlabel('Number of Words in Article', fontsize=14)
>>> ax1.set_ylabel('Number of Articles', fontsize=14)

>>> df['log_n_tokens_content'].hist(ax=ax2, bins=100)
>>> ax2.tick_params(labelsize=14)
>>> ax2.set_xlabel('Log of Number of Words', fontsize=14)
>>> ax2.set_ylabel('Number of Articles', fontsize=14)
```

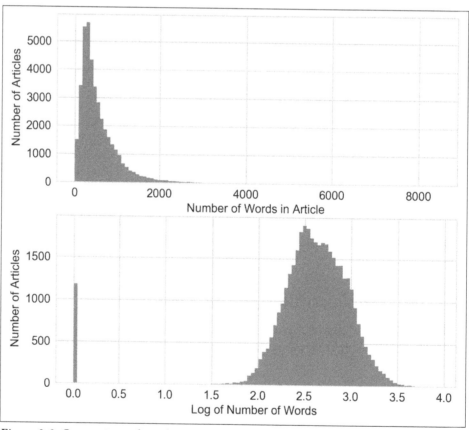

Figure 2-8. Comparison of word counts in Mashable news articles before (top) and after (bottom) log transformation

Log Transform in Action

Let's see how the log transform performs for supervised learning. We'll use both of the previous datasets here. For the Yelp reviews dataset, we'll use the number of reviews to predict the average rating of a business (see Example 2-8). For the Mashable news articles, we'll use the number of words in an article to predict its popularity. Since the outputs are continuous numbers, we'll use simple linear regression as the model. We use scikit-learn (*http://scikit-learn.org/*) to perform 10-fold cross validation of linear regression on the feature with and without log transformation. The models are evaluated by the R-squared score (*http://bit.ly/2D4ZKap*), which measures how well a trained regression model predicts new data. Good models have high R-squared scores. A perfect model gets the maximum score of 1. The score can be negative, and a bad model can get an arbitrarily low negative score. Using cross validation, we obtain not only an estimate of the score but also a variance, which helps us gauge whether the differences between the two models are meaningful.

Example 2-8. Using log transformed Yelp review counts to predict average business rating

```
>>> import pandas as pd
>>> import numpy as np
>>> import json
>>> from sklearn import linear_model
>>> from sklearn.model_selection import cross_val_score

# Using the previously loaded Yelp reviews DataFrame,
# compute the log transform of the Yelp review count.
# Note that we add 1 to the raw count to prevent the logarithm from
# exploding into negative infinity in case the count is zero.
>>> biz_df['log_review_count'] = np.log10(biz_df['review_count'] + 1)

# Train linear regression models to predict the average star rating of a business,
# using the review_count feature with and without log transformation.
# Compare the 10-fold cross validation score of the two models.
>>> m_orig = linear_model.LinearRegression()
>>> scores_orig = cross_val_score(m_orig, biz_df[['review_count']],
...                               biz_df['stars'], cv=10)
>>> m_log = linear_model.LinearRegression()
>>> scores_log = cross_val_score(m_log, biz_df[['log_review_count']],
...                              biz_df['stars'], cv=10)
>>> print("R-squared score without log transform: %0.5f (+/- %0.5f)"
...       % (scores_orig.mean(), scores_orig.std() * 2))
>>> print("R-squared score with log transform: %0.5f (+/- %0.5f)"
...       % (scores_log.mean(), scores_log.std() * 2))
R-squared score without log transform: -0.03683 (+/- 0.07280)
R-squared score with log transform: -0.03694 (+/- 0.07650)
```

Judging by the output of the experiment, the two simple models (with and without log transform) are equally bad at predicting the target, with the log transformed feature performing slightly worse. How disappointing! It's not surprising that neither of them are very good, given that they both use just one feature, but one would have hoped that the log transformed feature might have performed better.

Now let's look at how the log transform does on the Online News Popularity dataset (Example 2-9).

Example 2-9. Using log transformed word counts in the Online News Popularity dataset to predict article popularity

```
# Download the Online News Popularity dataset from UCI, then use
# Pandas to load the file into a DataFrame.
>>> df = pd.read_csv('OnlineNewsPopularity.csv', delimiter=', ')

# Take the log transform of the 'n_tokens_content' feature, which
# represents the number of words (tokens) in a news article.
>>> df['log_n_tokens_content'] = np.log10(df['n_tokens_content'] + 1)

# Train two linear regression models to predict the number of shares
# of an article, one using the original feature and the other the
# log transformed version.
>>> m_orig = linear_model.LinearRegression()
>>> scores_orig = cross_val_score(m_orig, df[['n_tokens_content']],
...                                df['shares'], cv=10)
>>> m_log = linear_model.LinearRegression()
>>> scores_log = cross_val_score(m_log, df[['log_n_tokens_content']],
...                               df['shares'], cv=10)
>>> print("R-squared score without log transform: %0.5f (+/- %0.5f)"
...       % (scores_orig.mean(), scores_orig.std() * 2))
>>> print("R-squared score with log transform: %0.5f (+/- %0.5f)"
...       % (scores_log.mean(), scores_log.std() * 2))
R-squared score without log transform: -0.00242 (+/- 0.00509)
R-squared score with log transform: -0.00114 (+/- 0.00418)
```

The confidence intervals still overlap, but the model with the log transformed feature is doing better than the one without. Why is the log transform so much more successful on this dataset? We can get a clue by looking at the scatter plots (Example 2-10) of the input feature and target values. As can be seen in the bottom panel of Figure 2-9, the log transform reshaped the x-axis, pulling the articles with large outliers in the target value (>200,000 shares) further out toward the righthand side of the axis. This gives the linear model more "breathing room" on the low end of the input feature space. Without the log transform (top panel), the model is under more pressure to fit very different target values under very small changes in the input.

Example 2-10. Visualizing the correlation between input and output in the news popularity prediction problem

```
>>> fig2, (ax1, ax2) = plt.subplots(2,1)
>>> ax1.scatter(df['n_tokens_content'], df['shares'])
>>> ax1.tick_params(labelsize=14)
>>> ax1.set_xlabel('Number of Words in Article', fontsize=14)
>>> ax1.set_ylabel('Number of Shares', fontsize=14)

>>> ax2.scatter(df['log_n_tokens_content'], df['shares'])
>>> ax2.tick_params(labelsize=14)
>>> ax2.set_xlabel('Log of the Number of Words in Article', fontsize=14)
>>> ax2.set_ylabel('Number of Shares', fontsize=14)
```

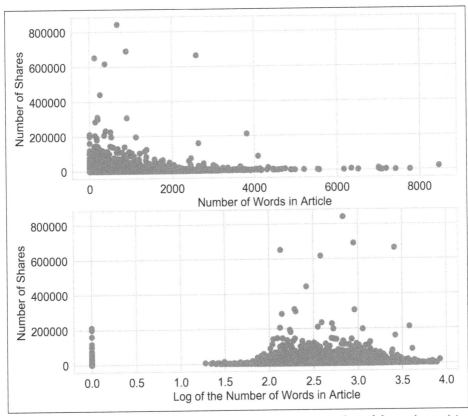

Figure 2-9. Scatter plots of number of words (input) versus number of shares (target) in the Online News Popularity dataset—the top plot visualizes the original feature, and the bottom plot shows the scatter plot after log transformation

Compare this with the same scatter plot applied to the Yelp reviews dataset (Example 2-11). Figure 2-10 looks very different from Figure 2-9. The average star rating is discretized in increments of half-stars ranging from 1 to 5. High review counts (roughly >2,500 reviews) do correlate with higher average star ratings, but the relationship is far from linear. There is no clear way to draw a line to predict the average star rating based on either input. Essentially, the plot shows that review count and its logarithm are both bad linear predictors of average star rating.

Example 2-11. Visualizing the correlation between input and output in Yelp business review prediction

```
>>> fig, (ax1, ax2) = plt.subplots(2,1)
>>> ax1.scatter(biz_df['review_count'], biz_df['stars'])
>>> ax1.tick_params(labelsize=14)
>>> ax1.set_xlabel('Review Count', fontsize=14)
>>> ax1.set_ylabel('Average Star Rating', fontsize=14)

>>> ax2.scatter(biz_df['log_review_count'], biz_df['stars'])
>>> ax2.tick_params(labelsize=14)
>>> ax2.set_xlabel('Log of Review Count', fontsize=14)
>>> ax2.set_ylabel('Average Star Rating', fontsize=14)
```

The Importance of Data Visualization

The comparison of the effect of the log transform on two different datasets illustrates the importance of visualizing the data. Here, we intentionally kept the input and target variables simple so that we can easily visualize the relationship between them. Plots like those in Figure 2-10 immediately reveal that the chosen model (linear) cannot possibly represent the relationship between the chosen input and target. On the other hand, one could convincingly model the distribution of review count *given* the average star rating. When building models, it is a good idea to visually inspect the relationships between input and output, and between different input features.

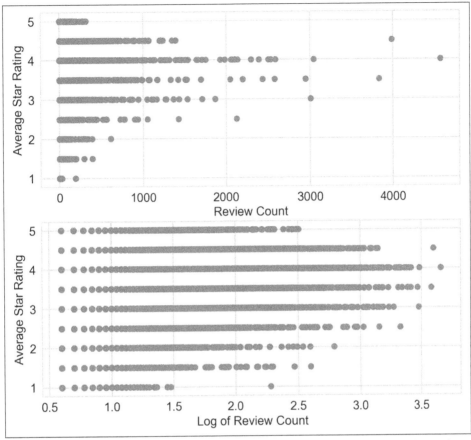

Figure 2-10. Scatter plots of review counts (input) versus average star rating (target) in the Yelp reviews dataset—the top panel plots the original review count, and the bottom panel plots the review count after log transformation

Power Transforms: Generalization of the Log Transform

The log transform is a specific example of a family of transformations known as *power transforms*. In statistical terms, these are *variance-stabilizing transformations*. To understand why variance stabilization is good, consider the Poisson distribution. This is a heavy-tailed distribution with a variance that is equal to its mean: hence, the larger its center of mass, the larger its variance, and the heavier the tail. Power transforms change the distribution of the variable so that the variance is no longer dependent on the mean. For example, suppose a random variable X has the Poisson distribution. If we transform X by taking its square root, the variance of $\tilde{X} = \sqrt{X}$ is roughly constant, instead of being equal to the mean.

Figure 2-11 illustrates λ, which represents the mean of the distribution. As λ increases, not only does the mode of the distribution shift to the right, but the mass spreads out and the variance becomes larger.

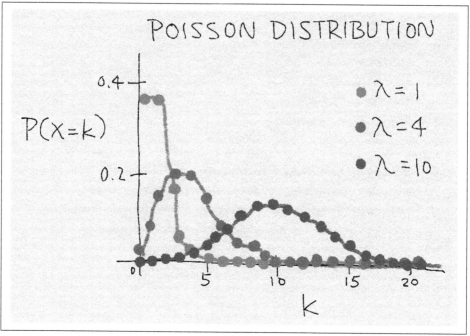

Figure 2-11. A rough illustration of the Poisson distribution, an example distribution where the variance increases along with the mean

A simple generalization of both the square root transform and the log transform is known as the Box-Cox transform:

$$\tilde{x} = \begin{cases} \dfrac{x^{\lambda} - 1}{\lambda} & \text{if } \lambda \neq 0, \\ \ln(x) & \text{if } \lambda = 0. \end{cases}$$

Figure 2-12 shows the Box-Cox transform for λ = 0 (the log transform), λ = 0.25, λ = 0.5 (a scaled and shifted version of the square root transform), λ = 0.75, and λ = 1.5. Setting λ to be less than 1 compresses the higher values, and setting λ higher than 1 has the opposite effect.

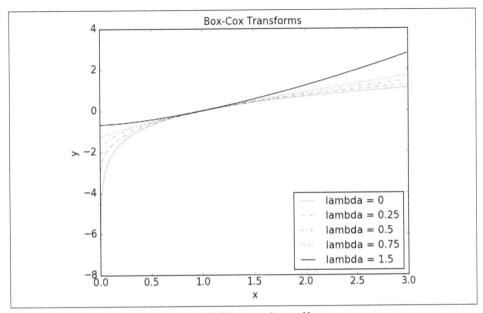

Figure 2-12. Box-Cox transforms for different values of λ

The Box-Cox formulation only works when the data is positive. For nonpositive data, one could shift the values by adding a fixed constant. When applying the Box-Cox transformation or a more general power transform, we have to determine a value for the parameter λ. This may be done via maximum likelihood (finding the λ that maximizes the Gaussian likelihood of the resulting transformed signal) or Bayesian methods. A full treatment of the usage of Box-Cox and general power transforms is outside the scope of this book. Interested readers may find more information on power transforms in *Econometric Methods* by Johnston and DiNardo (1997). Fortunately, SciPy's `stats` package (*https://docs.scipy.org/doc/scipy/reference/stats.html*) contains an implementation of the Box-Cox transformation that includes finding the optimal transform parameter. Example 2-12 demonstrates its use on the Yelp reviews dataset.

Example 2-12. Box-Cox transformation of Yelp business review counts

```
>>> from scipy import stats

# Continuing from the previous example, assume biz_df contains
# the Yelp business reviews data.
# The Box-Cox transform assumes that input data is positive.
# Check the min to make sure.
>>> biz_df['review_count'].min()
3
```

```
# Setting input parameter lmbda to 0 gives us the log transform (without
# constant offset)
>>> rc_log = stats.boxcox(biz_df['review_count'], lmbda=0)
# By default, the scipy implementation of Box-Cox transform finds the lambda
# parameter that will make the output the closest to a normal distribution
>>> rc_bc, bc_params = stats.boxcox(biz_df['review_count'])
>>> bc_params
-0.4106510862321085
```

Figure 2-13 provides a visual comparison of the distributions of the original and transformed counts (see Example 2-13).

Example 2-13. Visualizing the histograms of original, log transformed, and Box-Cox transformed counts

```
>>> fig, (ax1, ax2, ax3) = plt.subplots(3,1)
# original review count histogram
>>> biz_df['review_count'].hist(ax=ax1, bins=100)
>>> ax1.set_yscale('log')
>>> ax1.tick_params(labelsize=14)
>>> ax1.set_title('Review Counts Histogram', fontsize=14)
>>> ax1.set_xlabel('')
>>> ax1.set_ylabel('Occurrence', fontsize=14)

# review count after log transform
>>> biz_df['rc_log'].hist(ax=ax2, bins=100)
>>> ax2.set_yscale('log')
>>> ax2.tick_params(labelsize=14)
>>> ax2.set_title('Log Transformed Counts Histogram', fontsize=14)
>>> ax2.set_xlabel('')
>>> ax2.set_ylabel('Occurrence', fontsize=14)

# review count after optimal Box-Cox transform
>>> biz_df['rc_bc'].hist(ax=ax3, bins=100)
>>> ax3.set_yscale('log')
>>> ax3.tick_params(labelsize=14)
>>> ax3.set_title('Box-Cox Transformed Counts Histogram', fontsize=14)
>>> ax3.set_xlabel('')
>>> ax3.set_ylabel('Occurrence', fontsize=14)
```

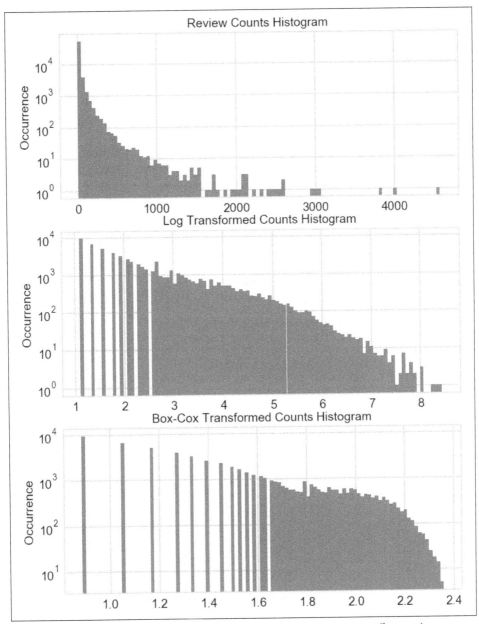

Figure 2-13. Box-Cox transformation of Yelp business review counts (bottom), compared to original (top) and log transformed (middle) histograms

A *probability plot*, or probplot, is an easy way to visually compare an empirical distribution of data against a theoretical distribution. This is essentially a scatter plot of observed versus theoretical quantiles. Figure 2-14 shows the probplots of original and transformed Yelp review counts data against the normal distribution (see Example 2-14). Since the observed data is strictly positive and the Gaussian can be negative, the quantiles could never match up on the negative end. Thus, our focus is on the positive side. On this front, the original counts are obviously much more heavy-tailed than a normal distribution. (The ordered values go up to 4,000, whereas the theoretical quantiles only stretch to 4.) Both the plain log transform and the optimal Box-Cox transform bring the positive tail closer to normal. The optimal Box-Cox transform deflates the tail more than the log transform, as is evident from the fact that the tail flattens out under the red diagonal equivalence line.

Example 2-14. Probability plots of original and transformed counts against the normal distribution

```
>>> fig2, (ax1, ax2, ax3) = plt.subplots(3,1)
>>> prob1 = stats.probplot(biz_df['review_count'], dist=stats.norm, plot=ax1)
>>> ax1.set_xlabel('')
>>> ax1.set_title('Probplot against normal distribution')
>>> prob2 = stats.probplot(biz_df['rc_log'], dist=stats.norm, plot=ax2)
>>> ax2.set_xlabel('')
>>> ax2.set_title('Probplot after log transform')
>>> prob3 = stats.probplot(biz_df['rc_bc'], dist=stats.norm, plot=ax3)
>>> ax3.set_xlabel('Theoretical quantiles')
>>> ax3.set_title('Probplot after Box-Cox transform')
```

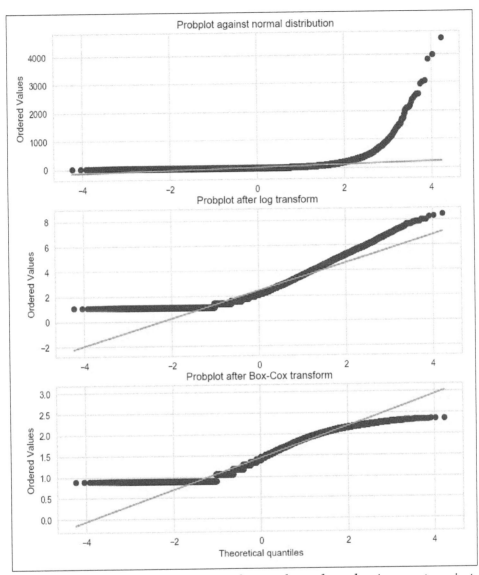

Figure 2-14. Comparing the distribution of raw and transformed review counts against the normal distribution

Feature Scaling or Normalization

Some features, such as latitude or longitude, are bounded in value. Other numeric features, such as counts, may increase without bound. Models that are smooth functions of the input, such as linear regression, logistic regression, or anything that involves a matrix, are affected by the scale of the input. Tree-based models, on the other hand, couldn't care less. If your model is sensitive to the scale of input features, feature scaling could help. As the name suggests, feature scaling changes the scale of the feature. Sometimes people also call it *feature normalization*. Feature scaling is usually done individually to each feature. Next, we will discuss several types of common scaling operations, each resulting in a different distribution of feature values.

Min-Max Scaling

Let x be an individual feature value (i.e., a value of the feature in some data point), and $\min(x)$ and $\max(x)$, respectively, be the minimum and maximum values of this feature over the entire dataset. Min-max scaling squeezes (or stretches) all feature values to be within the range of [0, 1]. Figure 2-15 demonstrates this concept. The formula for min-max scaling is:

$$\tilde{x} = \frac{x - \min(x)}{\max(x) - \min(x)}$$

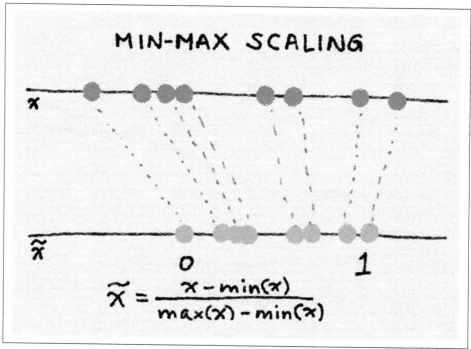

Figure 2-15. Illustration of min-max scaling

Standardization (Variance Scaling)

Feature standardization is defined as:

$$\tilde{x} = \frac{x - \text{mean}(x)}{\text{sqrt}(\text{var}(x))}$$

It subtracts off the mean of the feature (over all data points) and divides by the variance. Hence, it can also be called *variance scaling*. The resulting scaled feature has a mean of 0 and a variance of 1. If the original feature has a Gaussian distribution, then the scaled feature does too. Figure 2-16 is an illustration of standardization.

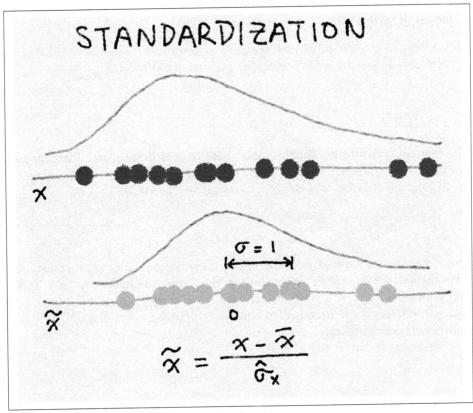

Figure 2-16. Illustration of feature standardization

Don't "Center" Sparse Data!

Use caution when performing min-max scaling and standardization on sparse features. Both subtract a quantity from the original feature value. For min-max scaling, the shift is the minimum over all values of the current feature; for standardization, it is the mean. If the shift is not zero, then these two transforms can turn a sparse feature vector where most values are zero into a dense one. This in turn could create a huge computational burden for the classifier, depending on how it is implemented (not to mention that it would be horrendous if the representation now included every word that didn't appear in a document!). Bag-of-words is a sparse representation, and most classification libraries optimize for sparse inputs.

ℓ^2 Normalization

This technique normalizes (divides) the original feature value by what's known as the ℓ^2 norm, also known as the Euclidean norm. It's defined as follows:

$$\tilde{x} = \frac{x}{\| x \|_2}$$

The ℓ^2 norm measures the length of the vector in coordinate space. The definition can be derived from the well-known Pythagorean theorem that gives us the length of the hypotenuse of a right triangle given the lengths of the sides:

$$\| x \|_2 = \sqrt{x_1^2 + x_2^2 + \ldots + x_m^2}$$

The ℓ^2 norm sums the squares of the values of the features across data points, then takes the square root. After ℓ^2 normalization, the feature column has norm 1. This is also sometimes called ℓ^2 scaling. (Loosely speaking, *scaling* means multiplying by a constant, whereas *normalization* could involve a number of operations.) Figure 2-17 illustrates ℓ^2 normalization.

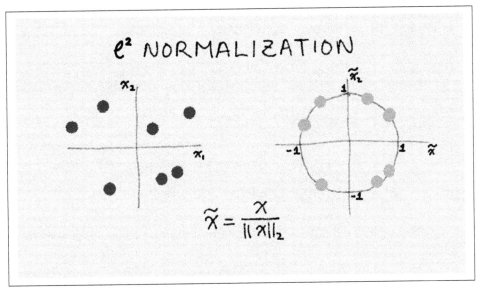

$$\tilde{x} = \frac{x}{\|x\|_2}$$

Figure 2-17. Illustration of ℓ^2 feature normalization

Data Space Versus Feature Space

Note that the illustration in Figure 2-17 is in data space, not feature space. One can also do ℓ^2 normalization for the data point instead of the feature, which will result in data vectors with unit norm (norm of 1). See the discussion in "Bag-of-Words" on page 42 about the complementary nature of data vectors and feature vectors.

No matter the scaling method, feature scaling always divides the feature by a constant (known as the *normalization constant*). Therefore, it does not change the shape of the single-feature distribution. We'll illustrate this with the online news article token counts (see Example 2-15).

Example 2-15. Feature scaling example

```
>>> import pandas as pd
>>> import sklearn.preprocessing as preproc

# Load the Online News Popularity dataset
>>> df = pd.read_csv('OnlineNewsPopularity.csv', delimiter=', ')

# Look at the original data - the number of words in an article
>>> df['n_tokens_content'].as_matrix()
array([ 219.,  255.,  211., ...,  442.,  682.,  157.])

# Min-max scaling
>>> df['minmax'] = preproc.minmax_scale(df[['n_tokens_content']])
```

```
>>> df['minmax'].as_matrix()
array([ 0.02584376, 0.03009205, 0.02489969, ..., 0.05215955,
        0.08048147, 0.01852726])

# Standardization - note that by definition, some outputs will be negative
>>> df['standardized'] = preproc.StandardScaler().fit_transform(df[['n_tokens_content']])
>>> df['standardized'].as_matrix()
array([-0.69521045, -0.61879381, -0.71219192, ..., -0.2218518 ,
        0.28759248, -0.82681689])

# L2-normalization
>>> df['l2_normalized'] = preproc.normalize(df[['n_tokens_content']], axis=0)
>>> df['l2_normalized'].as_matrix()
array([ 0.00152439, 0.00177498, 0.00146871, ..., 0.00307663,
        0.0047472 , 0.00109283])
```

We can also visualize the distribution of data with different feature scaling methods (Figure 2-18). As Example 2-16 shows, unlike the log transform, feature scaling doesn't change the shape of the distribution; only the scale of the data changes.

Example 2-16. Plotting the histograms of original and scaled data

```
>>> fig, (ax1, ax2, ax3, ax4) = plt.subplots(4,1)
>>> fig.tight_layout()
>>> df['n_tokens_content'].hist(ax=ax1, bins=100)
>>> ax1.tick_params(labelsize=14)
>>> ax1.set_xlabel('Article word count', fontsize=14)
>>> ax1.set_ylabel('Number of articles', fontsize=14)

>>> df['minmax'].hist(ax=ax2, bins=100)
>>> ax2.tick_params(labelsize=14)
>>> ax2.set_xlabel('Min-max scaled word count', fontsize=14)
>>> ax2.set_ylabel('Number of articles', fontsize=14)

>>> df['standardized'].hist(ax=ax3, bins=100)
>>> ax3.tick_params(labelsize=14)
>>> ax3.set_xlabel('Standardized word count', fontsize=14)
>>> ax3.set_ylabel('Number of articles', fontsize=14)

>>> df['l2_normalized'].hist(ax=ax4, bins=100)
>>> ax4.tick_params(labelsize=14)
>>> ax4.set_xlabel('L2-normalized word count', fontsize=14)
>>> ax4.set_ylabel('Number of articles', fontsize=14)
```

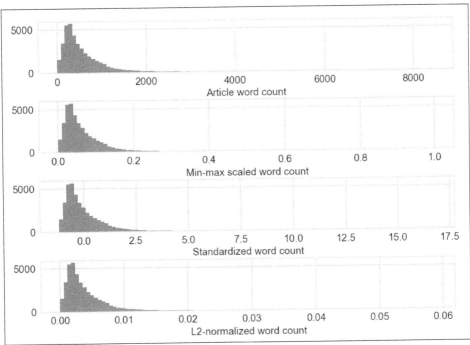

Figure 2-18. Original and scaled news article word counts—note that only the scale of the x-axis changes; the shape of the distribution stays the same with feature scaling

Feature scaling is useful in situations where a set of input features differs wildly in scale. For instance, the number of daily visitors to a popular ecommerce site might be a hundred thousand, while the actual number of sales might be in the thousands. If both of those features are thrown into a model, then the model will need to balance its scale while figuring out what to do. Drastically varying scale in input features can lead to numeric stability issues for the model training algorithm. In those situations, it's a good idea to standardize the features. Chapter 4 goes into detail about feature scaling in the context of handling natural text, including usage examples.

Interaction Features

A simple pairwise *interaction feature* is the product of two features. The analogy is the logical AND. It expresses the outcome in terms of pairs of conditions: "the purchase is coming from zip code 98121" AND "the user's age is between 18 and 35." Decision tree–based models get this for free, but generalized linear models often find interaction features very helpful.

A simple linear model uses a linear combination of the individual input features x_1, $x_2, ... x_n$ to predict the outcome y:

$$y = w_1x_1 + w_2x_2 + \ldots + w_nx_n$$

An easy way to extend the linear model is to include combinations of pairs of input features, like so:

$$y = w_1x_1 + w_2x_2 + \ldots + w_nx_n + w_{1,1}x_1x_1 + w_{1,2}x_1x_2 + w_{1,3}x_1x_3 + \ldots$$

This allows us to capture interactions between features, and hence these pairs are called *interaction features*. If x_1 and x_2 are binary, then their product x_1x_2 is the logical function x_1 AND x_2. Suppose the problem is to predict a customer's preference based on their profile information. In our example, instead of making predictions based solely on the age or location of the user, interaction features allow the model to make predictions based on the user being of a certain age AND at a particular location.

In Example 2-17, we use pairwise interaction features from the UCI Online News Popularity dataset to predict the number of shares for each news article. As the results show, interaction features result in some lift in accuracy above singleton features. Both perform better than Example 2-9, which used as a single predictor the number of words in the body of the article (with or without a log transform).

Example 2-17. Example of interaction features in prediction

```
>>> from sklearn import linear_model
>>> from sklearn.model_selection import train_test_split
>>> import sklearn.preprocessing as preproc

# Assume df is a Pandas DataFrame containing the UCI Online News Popularity dataset
>>> df.columns
Index(['url', 'timedelta', 'n_tokens_title', 'n_tokens_content',
       'n_unique_tokens', 'n_non_stop_words', 'n_non_stop_unique_tokens',
       'num_hrefs', 'num_self_hrefs', 'num_imgs', 'num_videos',
       'average_token_length', 'num_keywords', 'data_channel_is_lifestyle',
       'data_channel_is_entertainment', 'data_channel_is_bus',
       'data_channel_is_socmed', 'data_channel_is_tech',
       'data_channel_is_world', 'kw_min_min', 'kw_max_min', 'kw_avg_min',
       'kw_min_max', 'kw_max_max', 'kw_avg_max', 'kw_min_avg', 'kw_max_avg',
       'kw_avg_avg', 'self_reference_min_shares', 'self_reference_max_shares',
       'self_reference_avg_sharess', 'weekday_is_monday', 'weekday_is_tuesday',
       'weekday_is_wednesday', 'weekday_is_thursday', 'weekday_is_friday',
       'weekday_is_saturday', 'weekday_is_sunday', 'is_weekend', 'LDA_00',
       'LDA_01', 'LDA_02', 'LDA_03', 'LDA_04', 'global_subjectivity',
       'global_sentiment_polarity', 'global_rate_positive_words',
       'global_rate_negative_words', 'rate_positive_words',
       'rate_negative_words', 'avg_positive_polarity', 'min_positive_polarity',
       'max_positive_polarity', 'avg_negative_polarity',
       'min_negative_polarity', 'max_negative_polarity', 'title_subjectivity',
       'title_sentiment_polarity', 'abs_title_subjectivity',
```

```
                'abs_title_sentiment_polarity', 'shares'],
            dtype='object')

# Select the content-based features as singleton features in the model,
# skipping over the derived features
>>> features = ['n_tokens_title', 'n_tokens_content',
...              'n_unique_tokens', 'n_non_stop_words', 'n_non_stop_unique_tokens',
...              'num_hrefs', 'num_self_hrefs', 'num_imgs', 'num_videos',
...              'average_token_length', 'num_keywords', 'data_channel_is_lifestyle',
...              'data_channel_is_entertainment', 'data_channel_is_bus',
...              'data_channel_is_socmed', 'data_channel_is_tech',
...              'data_channel_is_world']

>>> X = df[features]
>>> y = df[['shares']]

# Create pairwise interaction features, skipping the constant bias term
>>> X2 = preproc.PolynomialFeatures(include_bias=False).fit_transform(X)
>>> X2.shape
(39644, 170)

# Create train/test sets for both feature sets
>>> X1_train, X1_test, X2_train, X2_test, y_train, y_test = \
...     train_test_split(X, X2, y, test_size=0.3, random_state=123)

>>> def evaluate_feature(X_train, X_test, y_train, y_test):
...     """Fit a linear regression model on the training set and
...     score on the test set"""
...     model = linear_model.LinearRegression().fit(X_train, y_train)
...     r_score = model.score(X_test, y_test)
...     return (model, r_score)

# Train models and compare score on the two feature sets
>>> (m1, r1) = evaluate_feature(X1_train, X1_test, y_train, y_test)
>>> (m2, r2) = evaluate_feature(X2_train, X2_test, y_train, y_test)
>>> print("R-squared score with singleton features: %0.5f" % r1)
>>> print("R-squared score with pairwise features: %0.10f" % r2)
R-squared score with singleton features: 0.00924
R-squared score with pairwise features: 0.0113276523
```

Interaction features are very simple to formulate, but they are expensive to use. The training and scoring time of a linear model with pairwise interaction features would go from $O(n)$ to $O(n^2)$, where n is the number of singleton features.

There are a few ways around the computational expense of higher-order interaction features. One could perform feature selection on top of all of the interaction features. Alternatively, one could more carefully craft a smaller number of complex features.

Both strategies have their advantages and disadvantages. Feature selection employs computational means to select the best features for a problem. (This technique is not limited to interaction features.) However, some feature selection techniques still require training multiple models with a large number of features.

Handcrafted complex features can be expressive enough that only a small number of them are needed, which reduces the training time of the model—but the features themselves may be expensive to compute, which increases the computational cost of the model scoring stage. Good examples of handcrafted (or machine-learned) complex features may be found in Chapter 8. Let's now look at some feature selection techniques.

Feature Selection

Feature selection techniques prune away nonuseful features in order to reduce the complexity of the resulting model. The end goal is a parsimonious model that is quicker to compute, with little or no degradation in predictive accuracy. In order to arrive at such a model, some feature selection techniques require training more than one candidate model. In other words, feature selection is not about reducing training time—in fact, some techniques *increase* overall training time—but about reducing model scoring time.

Roughly speaking, feature selection techniques fall into three classes:

Filtering

Filtering techniques preprocess features to remove ones that are unlikely to be useful for the model. For example, one could compute the correlation or mutual information between each feature and the response variable, and filter out the features that fall below a threshold. Chapter 3 discusses examples of these techniques for text features. Filtering techniques are much cheaper than the wrapper techniques described next, but they do not take into account the model being employed. Hence, they may not be able to select the right features for the model. It is best to do prefiltering conservatively, so as not to inadvertently eliminate useful features before they even make it to the model training step.

Wrapper methods

These techniques are expensive, but they allow you to try out subsets of features, which means you won't accidentally prune away features that are uninformative by themselves but useful when taken in combination. The wrapper method treats the model as a black box that provides a quality score of a proposed subset for features. There is a separate method that iteratively refines the subset.

Embedded methods

These methods perform feature selection as part of the model training process. For example, a decision tree inherently performs feature selection because it selects one feature on which to split the tree at each training step. Another example is the ℓ^1 regularizer, which can be added to the training objective of any linear model. The ℓ^1 regularizer encourages models that use a few features as opposed to a lot of features, so it's also known as a sparsity constraint on the model. Embedded methods incorporate feature selection as part of the model training process. They are not as powerful as wrapper methods, but they are nowhere near as expensive. Compared to filtering, embedded methods select features that are specific to the model. In this sense, embedded methods strike a balance between computational expense and quality of results.

A full treatment of feature selection is outside the scope of this book. Interested readers may refer to the survey paper by Guyon and Elisseeff (2003).

Summary

This chapter discussed a number of common numeric feature engineering techniques, such as quantization, scaling (a.k.a. normalization), log transforms (a type of power transform), and interaction features, and gave a brief summary of feature selection techniques, necessary for handling large quantities of interaction features. In statistical machine learning, all data eventually boils down to numeric features. Therefore, all roads lead to some kind of numeric feature engineering technique at the end. Keep these tools handy for the end game of feature engineering!

Bibliography

Bertin-Mahieux, Thierry, Daniel P.W. Ellis, Brian Whitman, and Paul Lamere. "The Million Song Dataset." *Proceedings of the 12th International Society for Music Information Retrieval Conference* (2011): 591–596.

Fernandes, K., P. Vinagre, and P. Cortez. "A Proactive Intelligent Decision Support System for Predicting the Popularity of Online News." *Proceedings of the 17th Portuguese Conference on Artificial Intelligence* (2015): 535–546.

Guyon, Isabell, and André Elisseeff. "An Introduction to Variable and Feature Selection." *Journal of Machine Learning Research Special Issue on Variable and Feature Selection* 3 (2003): 1157–1182.

Johnston, Jack, and John DiNardo. *Econometric Methods*. 4th ed. New York: McGraw Hill, 1997.

## CHAPTER 3

Text Data: Flattening, Filtering, and Chunking

What would you do if you were designing an algorithm to analyze the following paragraph of text?

> Emma knocked on the door. No answer. She knocked again and waited. There was a large maple tree next to the house. Emma looked up the tree and saw a giant raven perched at the treetop. Under the afternoon sun, the raven gleamed magnificently. Its beak was hard and pointed, its claws sharp and strong. It looked regal and imposing. It reigned the tree it stood on. The raven was looking straight at Emma with its beady black eyes. Emma felt slightly intimidated. She took a step back from the door and tentatively said, "Hello?"

The paragraph contains a lot of information. We know that it involves someone named Emma and a raven. There is a house and a tree, and Emma is trying to get into the house but sees the raven instead. The raven is magnificent and has noticed Emma, who is a little scared but is making an attempt at communication.

So, which parts of this trove of information are salient features that we should extract? To start with, it seems like a good idea to extract the names of the main characters, Emma and the raven. Next, it might also be good to note the setting of a house, a door, and a tree. And what about the descriptions of the raven? What about Emma's actions—knocking on the door, taking a step back, and saying hello?

This chapter introduces the basics of feature engineering for text. We start out with *bag-of-words*, which is the simplest representation based on word count statistics. A very much related transformation is *tf-idf*, which is essentially a feature scaling technique. It is pulled out into its own chapter (the next one) for a full discussion. The current chapter first talks about text extraction features, then delves into how to filter and clean those features.

Bag-of-X: Turning Natural Text into Flat Vectors

Whether constructing machine learning models or engineering features, it's nice when the result is simple and interpretable. Simple things are easy to try, and interpretable features and models are easier to debug than complex ones. Simple and interpretable features do not always lead to the most accurate model, but it's a good idea to start simple and only add complexity when absolutely necessary.

For text data, we can start with a list of word count statistics called a bag-of-words. A list of word counts makes no special effort to find the interesting entities, such as Emma or the raven. But those two words are repeatedly mentioned in our sample paragraph, and they have a higher count than a random word like "hello." For simple tasks such as classifying a document, word count statistics often suffice. This technique can also be used in information retrieval, where the goal is to retrieve the set of documents that are relevant to an input text query. Both tasks are well served by word-level features because the presence or absence of certain words is a great indicator of the topic content of the document.

Bag-of-Words

In bag-of-words (BoW) featurization, a text document is converted into a vector of counts. (A vector is just a collection of n numbers.) The vector contains an entry for every possible word in the vocabulary. If the word—say, "aardvark"—appears three times in the document, then the feature vector has a count of 3 in the position corresponding to that word. If a word in the vocabulary doesn't appear in the document, then it gets a count of 0. For example, the text "it is a puppy and it is extremely cute" has the BoW representation shown in Figure 3-1.

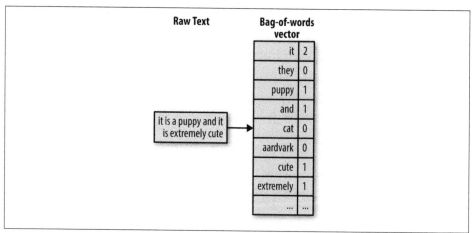

Figure 3-1. Turning raw text into a bag-of-words representation

Bag-of-words converts a text document into a flat vector. It is "flat" because it doesn't contain any of the original textual structures. The original text is a sequence of words. But a bag-of-words has no sequence; it just remembers how many times each word appears in the text. Thus, as Figure 3-2 demonstrates, the ordering of words in the vector is not important, as long as it is consistent for all documents in the dataset. Neither does bag-of-words represent any concept of word hierarchy. For example, the concept of "animal" includes "dog," "cat," "raven," etc. But in a bag-of-words representation, these words are all equal elements of the vector.

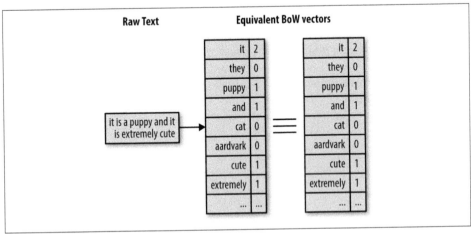

Figure 3-2. Two equivalent BoW vectors

What is important here is the geometry of data in feature space. In a bag-of-words vector, each word becomes a dimension of the vector. If there are n words in the vocabulary, then a document becomes a point[1] in n-dimensional space. It is difficult to visualize the geometry of anything beyond two or three dimensions, so we will have to use our imagination. Figure 3-3 shows what our example sentence looks like in the two-dimensional feature space corresponding to the words "puppy" and "cute."

---

1 Sometimes people use the term "document vector." The vector extends from the origin and ends at the specified point. For our purposes, "vector" and "point" are the same thing.

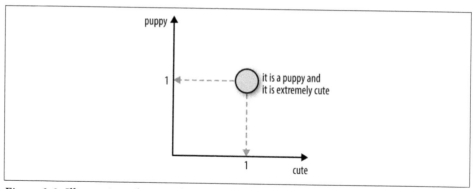

Figure 3-3. Illustration of a sample text document in a 2D feature space

Figure 3-4 shows three sentences in a 3D space corresponding to the words "puppy," "extremely," and "cute."

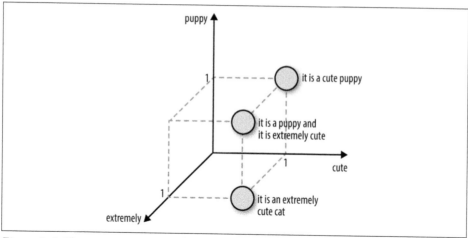

Figure 3-4. Three sentences in 3D feature space

These figures both depict data vectors in feature space. The axes denote individual words, which are features in the bag-of-words representation, and the points in space denote data points (text documents). Sometimes it is also informative to look at *feature* vectors in *data* space. A feature vector contains the value of the feature in each data point. The axes denote individual data points, and the points denote feature vectors. Figure 3-5 shows an example. With bag-of-words featurization for text documents, a feature is a word, and a feature vector contains the counts of this word in each document. In this way, a word is represented as a "bag-of-documents." As we shall see in Chapter 4, these bag-of-documents vectors come from the matrix transpose of the bag-of-words vectors.

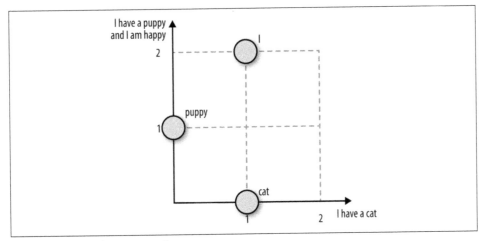

Figure 3-5. Word vectors in document space

Bag-of-words is not perfect. Breaking down a sentence into single words can destroy the semantic meaning. For instance, "not bad" semantically means "decent" or even "good" (especially if you're British). But "not" and "bad" constitute a floating negation plus a negative sentiment. "toy dog" and "dog toy" could be very different things (unless it's a dog toy of a toy dog), and the meaning is lost with the singleton words "toy" and "dog." It's easy to come up with many such examples. Bag-of-n-Grams, which we discuss next, alleviates some of the issue but is not a fundamental fix. It's good to keep in mind that bag-of-words is a simple and useful heuristic, but it is far from a correct semantic understanding of text.

Bag-of-n-Grams

Bag-of-n-Grams, or bag-of-n-grams, is a natural extension of bag-of-words. An n-gram is a sequence of n tokens. A word is essentially a 1-gram, also known as a *unigram*. After tokenization, the counting mechanism can collate individual tokens into word counts, or count overlapping sequences as n-grams. For example, the sentence "Emma knocked on the door" generates the n-grams "Emma knocked," "knocked on," "on the," and "the door."

n-grams retain more of the original sequence structure of the text, and therefore the bag-of-n-grams representation can be more informative. However, this comes at a cost. Theoretically, with k unique words, there could be k^2 unique 2-grams (also called *bigrams*). In practice, there are not nearly so many, because not every word can follow every other word. Nevertheless, there are usually a lot more distinct n-grams ($n > 1$) than words. This means that bag-of-n-grams is a much bigger and sparser feature space. It also means that n-grams are more expensive to compute, store, and model. The larger n is, the richer the information, and the greater the cost.

To illustrate how the number of *n*-grams grows with increasing *n* (see Figure 3-6), let's compute *n*-grams on the Yelp reviews dataset (*http://www.yelp.com/dataset_chal lenge*). In Example 3-1, we compute the *n*-grams of the first 10,000 reviews using Pandas and the `CountVectorizer` transformer in scikit-learn.

Example 3-1. Computing n-grams

```
>>> import pandas
>>> import json
>>> from sklearn.feature_extraction.text import CountVectorizer

# Load the first 10,000 reviews
>>> f = open('data/yelp/v6/yelp_academic_dataset_review.json')
>>> js = []
>>> for i in range(10000):
...     js.append(json.loads(f.readline()))
>>> f.close()
>>> review_df = pd.DataFrame(js)

# Create feature transformers for unigrams, bigrams, and trigrams.
# The default ignores single-character words, which is useful in practice because
# it trims uninformative words, but we explicitly include them in this example for
# illustration purposes.
>>> bow_converter = CountVectorizer(token_pattern='(?u)\\b\\w+\\b')
>>> bigram_converter = CountVectorizer(ngram_range=(2,2),
...                                    token_pattern='(?u)\\b\\w+\\b')
>>> trigram_converter = CountVectorizer(ngram_range=(3,3),
...                                     token_pattern='(?u)\\b\\w+\\b')

# Fit the transformers and look at vocabulary size
>>> bow_converter.fit(review_df['text'])
>>> words = bow_converter.get_feature_names()
>>> bigram_converter.fit(review_df['text'])
>>> bigrams = bigram_converter.get_feature_names()
>>> trigram_converter.fit(review_df['text'])
>>> trigrams = trigram_converter.get_feature_names()
>>> print (len(words), len(bigrams), len(trigrams))
26047 346301 847545

# Sneak a peek at the n-grams themselves
>>> words[:10]
['0', '00', '000', '0002', '00am', '00ish', '00pm', '01', '01am', '02']

>>> bigrams[-10:]
['zucchinis at',
 'zucchinis took',
 'zucchinis we',
 'zuma over',
 'zuppa di',
 'zuppa toscana',
 'zuppe di',
```

```
 'zurich and',
 'zz top',
 'à la']

>>> trigrams[:10]
['0 10 definitely',
 '0 2 also',
 '0 25 per',
 '0 3 miles',
 '0 30 a',
 '0 30 everything',
 '0 30 lb',
 '0 35 tip',
 '0 5 curry',
 '0 5 pork']
```

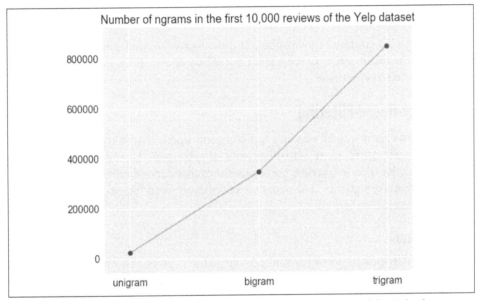

Figure 3-6. Number of unique n-grams in the first 10,000 reviews of the Yelp dataset

Filtering for Cleaner Features

With words, how do we cleanly separate the signal from the noise? Through filtering, techniques that use raw tokenization and counting to generate lists of simple words or *n*-grams become more usable. Phrase detection, which we will discuss next, can be seen as a particular bigram filter. Here are a few more ways to perform filtering.

Stopwords

Classification and retrieval do not usually require an in-depth understanding of the text. For instance, in the sentence "Emma knocked on the door," the words "on" and "the" don't change the fact that this sentence is about a person and a door. For coarse-grained tasks such as classification, the pronouns, articles, and prepositions may not add much value. The case may be very different in sentiment analysis, which requires a fine-grained understanding of semantics.

The popular Python NLP package NLTK (*http://www.nltk.org/*) contains a linguist-defined stopword list for many languages. (You will need to install NLTK and run `nltk.download()` to get all the goodies.) Various stopword lists can also be found on the web. For instance, here are some sample words from the English stopword list:

```
a, about, above, am, an, been, didn't, couldn't, i'd, i'll, itself, let's, myself,
our, they, through, when's, whom, ...
```

Note that the list contains apostrophes, and the words are uncapitalized. In order to use it as is, the tokenization process must not eat up apostrophes, and the words need to be converted to lowercase.

Frequency-Based Filtering

Stopword lists are a way of weeding out common words that make for vacuous features. There are other, more statistical ways of getting at the concept of "common words." In collocation extraction, we see methods that depend on manual definitions, and those that use statistics. The same idea applies to word filtering. We can use frequency statistics here as well.

Frequent words

Frequency statistics are great for filtering out corpus-specific common words as well as general-purpose stopwords. For instance, the phrase "New York Times" and each of the individual words in it appear frequently in the New York Times Annotated Corpus dataset (*https://catalog.ldc.upenn.edu/LDC2008T19*). Similarly, the word "house" appears often in the phrase "House of Commons" in the Hansard corpus (*http://www.hansard-corpus.org/*) of Canadian parliament debates, a dataset that is popularly used for statistical machine translation because it contains both an English and a French version of all documents. These words are meaningful in general, but not within those particular corpora. A typical stopword list will catch the general stopwords, but not corpus-specific ones.

Looking at the most frequent words can reveal parsing problems and highlight normally useful words that happen to appear too many times in the corpus. For example, Table 3-1 lists the 40 most frequent words in the Yelp reviews dataset. Here, frequency is based on the number of documents (reviews) they appear in, not their count within a document. As we can see, the list includes many stopwords. It also contains some surprises. "s" and "t" are on the list because we used the apostrophe as a tokenization delimiter, and words such as "Mary's" or "didn't" got parsed as "Mary s" and "didn t." Furthermore, the words "good," "food," and "great" each appear in around a third of the reviews, but we might want to keep them around because they are very useful for tasks such as sentiment analysis or business categorization.

Table 3-1. Most frequent words in the Yelp reviews dataset

Rank	Word	Document frequency	Rank	Word	Document frequency
1	the	1416058	21	t	684049
2	and	1381324	22	not	649824
3	a	1263126	23	s	626764
4	i	1230214	24	had	620284
5	to	1196238	25	so	608061
6	it	1027835	26	place	601918
7	of	1025638	27	good	598393
8	for	993430	28	at	596317
9	is	988547	29	are	585548
10	in	961518	30	food	562332
11	was	929703	31	be	543588
12	this	844824	32	we	537133
13	but	822313	33	great	520634
14	my	786595	34	were	516685
15	that	777045	35	there	510897
16	with	775044	36	here	481542
17	on	735419	37	all	478490
18	they	720994	38	if	475175
19	you	701015	39	very	460796
20	have	692749	40	out	460452

In practice, it helps to combine frequency-based filtering with a stopword list. There is also the tricky question of where to place the cutoff. Unfortunately there is no universal answer. Most of the time the cutoff needs to be determined manually, and may need to be reexamined when the dataset changes.

Rare words

Depending on the task, one might also need to filter out rare words. These might be truly obscure words, or misspellings of common words. To a statistical model, a word that appears in only one or two documents is more like noise than useful information. For example, suppose the task is to categorize businesses based on their Yelp reviews, and a single review contains the word "gobbledygook." How would one tell, based on this one word, whether the business is a restaurant, a beauty salon, or a bar? Even if we knew that the business in this case happened to be a bar, it would probably be a mistake to classify as such for other reviews that contain the word "gobbledygook."

Not only are rare words unreliable as predictors, they also generate computational overhead. The set of 1.6 million Yelp reviews contains 357,481 unique words (tokenized by space and punctuation characters), 189,915 of which appear in only one review, and 41,162 in two reviews. Over 60% of the vocabulary occurs rarely. This is a so-called *heavy-tailed distribution*, and it is very common in real-world data. The training time of many statistical machine learning models scales linearly with the number of features, and some models are quadratic or worse. Rare words incur a large computation and storage cost for not much additional gain.

Rare words can be easily identified and trimmed based on word count statistics. Alternatively, their counts can be aggregated into a special garbage bin, which can serve as an additional feature. Figure 3-7 demonstrates this representation on a short document that contains a bunch of usual words and two rare words, "gobbledygook" and "zylophant." The usual words retain their own counts, which can be further filtered by stopword lists or other frequency-based methods. The rare words lose their identity and get grouped into a garbage bin feature.

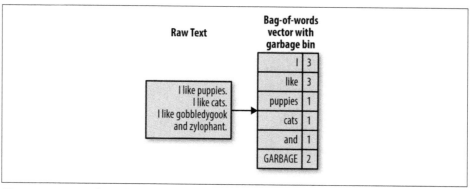

Figure 3-7. Bag-of-words feature vector with a garbage bin

Since one won't know which words are rare until the whole corpus has been counted, the garbage bin feature will need to be collected as a post-processing step.

Since this book is about feature engineering, our focus is on features. But the concept of rarity also applies to data points. If a text document is very short, then it likely contains no useful information and should not be used when training a model. One must use caution when applying this rule, however. The Wikipedia dump (*https://dumps.wikimedia.org/*) contains many pages that are incomplete stubs, which are probably safe to filter out. Tweets, on the other hand, are inherently short, and require other featurization and modeling tricks.

Stemming

One problem with simple parsing is that different variations of the same word get counted as separate words. For instance, "flower" and "flowers" are technically different tokens, and so are "swimmer," "swimming," and "swim," even though they are very close in meaning. It would be nice if all of these different variations got mapped to the same word.

Stemming is an NLP task that tries to chop each word down to its basic linguistic word stem form. There are different approaches. Some are based on linguistic rules, others on observed statistics. A subclass of algorithms incorporate part-of-speech tagging and linguistic rules in a process known as lemmatization.

Most stemming tools focus on the English language, though efforts are ongoing for other languages. The Porter stemmer (*http://tartarus.org/martin/PorterStemmer/*) is the most widely used free stemming tool for the English language. The original program is written in ANSI C, but many other packages have since wrapped it to provide access to other languages.

Here is an example of running the Porter stemmer through the NLTK Python package. As you can see, it handles a large number of cases, but it's not perfect. The word "goes" is mapped to "goe," while "go" is mapped to itself:

```
>>> import nltk
>>> stemmer = nltk.stem.porter.PorterStemmer()
>>> stemmer.stem('flowers')
u'flower'
>>> stemmer.stem('zeroes')
u'zero'
>>> stemmer.stem('stemmer')
u'stem'
>>> stemmer.stem('sixties')
u'sixti'
>>> stemmer.stem('sixty')
u'sixty'
>>> stemmer.stem('goes')
u'goe'
>>> stemmer.stem('go')
u'go'
```

Stemming does have a computation cost. Whether the end benefit outweighs the cost is application-dependent. It is also worth noting that stemming could hurt more than it helps. The words "new" and "news" have very different meanings, but both would be stemmed to "new." Similar examples abound. For this reason, stemming is not always used.

Atoms of Meaning: From Words to n-Grams to Phrases

The concept of bag-of-words is straightforward. But how does a computer know what a word is? A text document is represented digitally as a string, which is basically a sequence of characters. One might also run into semi-structured text in the form of JSON blobs or HTML pages. But even with the added tags and structure, the basic unit is still a string. How does one turn a string into a sequence of words? This involves the tasks of *parsing* and *tokenization*, which we discuss next.

Parsing and Tokenization

Parsing is necessary when the string contains more than plain text. For instance, if the raw data is a web page, an email, or a log of some sort, then it contains additional structure. One needs to decide how to handle the markup, the headers and footers, or the uninteresting sections of the log. If the document is a web page, then the parser needs to handle URLs. If it is an email, then fields like From, To, and Subject may require special handling—otherwise these headers will end up as normal words in the final count, which may not be useful.

After light parsing, the plain-text portion of the document can go through tokenization. This turns the string—a sequence of characters—into a sequence of tokens. Each token can then be counted as a word. The tokenizer needs to know what characters indicate that one token has ended and another is beginning. Space characters are usually good separators, as are punctuation characters. If the text contains tweets, then hash marks (#) should not be used as separators (also known as *delimiters*).

Sometimes, the analysis needs to operate on sentences instead of entire documents. For instance, *n*-grams, a generalization of the concept of a word, should not extend beyond sentence boundaries. More complex text featurization methods like word2vec also work with sentences or paragraphs. In these cases, one needs to first parse the document into sentences, then further tokenize each sentence into words.

String Objects: More Than Meets the Eye

String objects come in various encodings, like ASCII or Unicode. Plain English text can be encoded in ASCII. Most other languages require Unicode. If the document contains non-ASCII characters, then make sure that the tokenizer can handle that particular encoding. Otherwise, the results will be incorrect.

Collocation Extraction for Phrase Detection

A sequence of tokens immediately yields the list of words and *n*-grams. Semantically speaking, however, we are more used to understanding phrases, not *n*-grams. In computational natural language processing (NLP), the concept of a useful phrase is called a *collocation*. In the words of Manning and Schütze (1999: 151), "A collocation is an expression consisting of two or more words that correspond to some conventional way of saying things."

Collocations are more meaningful than the sum of their parts. For instance, "strong tea" has a different meaning beyond "great physical strength" and "tea"; therefore, it is considered a collocation. The phrase "cute puppy," on the other hand, means exactly the sum of its parts: "cute" and "puppy." Thus, it is not considered a collocation.

Collocations do not have to be consecutive sequences. For example, the sentence "Emma knocked on the door" is considered to contain the collocation "knock door." Hence, not every collocation is an n-gram. Conversely, not every n-gram is deemed a meaningful collocation.

Because collocations are more than the sum of their parts, their meaning cannot be adequately captured by individual word counts. Bag-of-words falls short as a representation. Bag-of-*n*-grams is also problematic because it captures too many meaningless sequences (consider "this is" in the bag-of-*n*-grams example) and not enough of the meaningful ones (i.e., knock door).

Collocations are useful as features. But how does one discover and extract them from text? One way is to predefine them. If we tried really hard, we could probably find comprehensive lists of idioms in various languages, and we could look through the text for any matches. It would be very expensive, but it would work. If the corpus is very domain specific and contains esoteric lingo, then this might be the preferred method. But the list would require a lot of manual curation, and it would need to be constantly updated for evolving corpora. For example, it probably wouldn't be very realistic for analyzing tweets, or for blogs and articles.

Since the advent of statistical NLP in the last two decades, people have opted more and more for statistical methods for finding phrases. Instead of establishing a fixed list of phrases and idiomatic sayings, statistical collocation extraction methods rely on the ever-evolving data to reveal the popular sayings of the day.

Frequency-based methods

A simple hack is to look at the most frequently occurring *n*-grams. The problem with this approach is that the most frequently occurring ones may not be the most useful ones. Table 3-2 shows the most popular bigrams ($n = 2$) in the entire Yelp reviews dataset. As we can see, the top 10 most frequently occurring bigrams by document count are very generic terms that don't contain much meaning.

Table 3-2. Most frequently occurring 2-grams in the Yelp reviews dataset

Bigram	Document count
of the	450,849
and the	426,346
in the	397,821
it was	396,713
this place	344,800
it s	341,090
and i	332,415
on the	325,044
i was	285,012
for the	276,946

Hypothesis testing for collocation extraction

Raw popularity count is too crude of a measure. We have to find more clever statistics to be able to pick out meaningful phrases easily. The key idea is to ask whether two words appear together more often than they would by chance. The statistical machinery for answering this question is called a *hypothesis test*.

Hypothesis testing is a way to boil noisy data down to "yes" or "no" answers. It involves modeling the data as samples drawn from random distributions. The randomness means that one can never be 100% sure about the answer; there's always the chance of an outlier. So, the answers are attached to a probability.

For example, the outcome of a hypothesis test might be "these two datasets come from the same distribution with 95% probability." For a gentle introduction to hypothesis testing, see the Khan Academy's tutorial on Hypothesis Testing and p-Values (*http://bit.ly/2G3bNIF*).

In the context of collocation extraction, many hypothesis tests have been proposed over the years. One of the most successful methods is based on the likelihood ratio test (Dunning, 1993). For a given pair of words, the method tests two hypotheses on the observed dataset. Hypothesis 1 (the null hypothesis) says that word 1 appears independently from word 2. Another way of saying this is that seeing word 1 has no bearing on whether we also see word 2. Hypothesis 2 (the alternate hypothesis) says that seeing word 1 changes the likelihood of seeing word 2. We take the alternate hypothesis to imply that the two words form a common phrase. Hence, the likelihood ratio test for phrase detection (a.k.a. collocation extraction) asks the following question: are the observed word occurrences in a given text corpus more likely to have been generated from a model where the two words occur independently from one another, or a model where the probabilities of the two words are entangled?

That is a mouthful. Let's math it up a little. (Math is great at expressing things very precisely and concisely, but it does require a completely different parser than natural language.)

We can express the null hypothesis H_{null} (independent) as $P(w_2 \mid w_1) = P(w_2 \mid \text{not } w_1)$, and the alternate hypothesis $H_{alternate}$ (not independent) as $P(w_2 \mid w_1) \neq P(w_2 \mid \text{not } w_1)$.

The final statistic is the log of the ratio between the two:

$$\log \lambda = \log \frac{L\,(\text{Data}; H_{null})}{L\,(\text{Data}; H_{alternate})}.$$

The likelihood function $L(Data; H)$ represents the probability of seeing the word frequencies in the dataset under the independent or the not independent model for the word pair. In order to compute this probability, we have to make another assumption about how the data is generated. The simplest data generation model is the binomial model, where for each word in the dataset, we toss a coin, and we insert our special word if the coin comes up heads, and some other word otherwise. Under this strategy, the count of the number of occurrences of the special word follows a *binomial distribution*. The binomial distribution is completely determined by the total number of words, the number of occurrences of the word of interest, and the heads probability.

The algorithm for detecting common phrases through likelihood ratio test analysis proceeds as follows:

1. Compute occurrence probabilities for all singleton words: $P(w)$.
2. Compute conditional pairwise word occurrence probabilities for all unique bigrams: $P(w_2 \mid w_1)$.
3. Compute the likelihood ratio $\log \lambda$ for all unique bigrams.
4. Sort the bigrams based on their likelihood ratio.
5. Take the bigrams with the smallest likelihood ratio values as features.

Getting a Grip on the Likelihood Ratio Test

The key is that what the test compares is not the probability parameters themselves, but rather the probability of seeing the observed data under those parameters (and an assumed data generation model). Likelihood is one of the key principles of statistical learning, but it is definitely a brain-twister the first few times you see it. Once you work out the logic, it becomes intuitive.

There is another statistical approach that's based on pointwise mutual information, but it is very sensitive to rare words, which are always present in real-world text corpora. Hence, it is not commonly used and we will not be demonstrating it here.

Note that all of the statistical methods for collocation extraction, whether using raw frequency, hypothesis testing, or pointwise mutual information, operate by filtering a list of candidate phrases. The easiest and cheapest way to generate such a list is by counting n-grams. It's possible to generate nonconsecutive sequences, but they are expensive to compute. In practice, even for consecutive n-grams, people rarely go beyond bigrams or trigrams because there are too many of them, even after filtering. To generate longer phrases, there are other methods such as chunking or combining with part-of-speech (PoS) tagging.

Chunking and part-of-speech tagging

Chunking is a bit more sophisticated than finding n-grams, in that it forms sequences of tokens based on parts of speech, using rule-based models.

For example, we might be most interested in finding all of the noun phrases in a problem where the entity (in this case the subject of a text) is the most interesting to us. In order to find this, we tokenize each word with a part of speech and then examine the token's neighborhood to look for part-of-speech groupings, or "chunks." The models that map words to parts of speech are generally language specific. Several open source Python libraries, such as NLTK, spaCy (*https://spacy.io/*), and TextBlob (*http://textblob.readthedocs.io/en/dev/*), have multiple language models available.

To illustrate how several libraries in Python make chunking using PoS tagging fairly straightforward, let's use the Yelp reviews dataset again. In Example 3-2, we evaluate the parts of speech to find the noun phrases using both spaCy and TextBlob.

Example 3-2. PoS tagging and chunking

```
>>> import pandas as pd
>>> import json

# Load the first 10 reviews
>>> f = open('data/yelp/v6/yelp_academic_dataset_review.json')
>>> js = []
>>> for i in range(10):
...     js.append(json.loads(f.readline()))
>>> f.close()
>>> review_df = pd.DataFrame(js)

# First we'll walk through spaCy's functions
>>> import spacy
# preload the language model
>>> nlp = spacy.load('en')
```

```
# We can create a Pandas Series of spaCy nlp variables
>>> doc_df = review_df['text'].apply(nlp)

# spaCy gives us fine-grained parts of speech using (.pos_)
# and coarse-grained parts of speech using (.tag_)
>>> for doc in doc_df[4]:
...     print([doc.text, doc.pos_, doc.tag_])

Got VERB VBP
a DET DT
letter NOUN NN
in ADP IN
the DET DT
mail NOUN NN
last ADJ JJ
week NOUN NN
that ADJ WDT
said VERB VBD
Dr. PROPN NNP
Goldberg PROPN NNP
is VERB VBZ
moving VERB VBG
to ADP IN
Arizona PROPN NNP
to PART TO
take VERB VB
a DET DT
new ADJ JJ
position NOUN NN
there ADV RB
in ADP IN
June PROPN NNP
. PUNCT .
  SPACE SP
He PRON PRP
will VERB MD
be VERB VB
missed VERB VBN
very ADV RB
much ADV RB
. PUNCT .


SPACE SP
I PRON PRP
think VERB VBP
finding VERB VBG
a DET DT
new ADJ JJ
doctor NOUN NN
in ADP IN
NYC PROPN NNP
```

```
that ADP IN
you PRON PRP
actually ADV RB
like INTJ UH
might VERB MD
almost ADV RB
be VERB VB
as ADV RB
awful ADJ JJ
as ADP IN
trying VERB VBG
to PART TO
find VERB VB
a DET DT
date NOUN NN
! PUNCT .


# spaCy also does some basic noun chunking for us
>>> print([chunk for chunk in doc_df[4].noun_chunks])
[a letter, the mail, Dr. Goldberg, Arizona, a new position, June, He, I,
a new doctor, NYC, you, a date]


#####
# We can do the same feature transformations using Textblob
from textblob import TextBlob

# The default tagger in TextBlob uses the PatternTagger, which is OK for our example.
# You can also specify the NLTK tagger, which works better for incomplete sentences.
>>> blob_df = review_df['text'].apply(TextBlob)

>>> blob_df[4].tags
[('Got', 'NNP'),
('a', 'DT'),
('letter', 'NN'),
('in', 'IN'),
('the', 'DT'),
('mail', 'NN'),
('last', 'JJ'),
('week', 'NN'),
('that', 'WDT'),
('said', 'VBD'),
('Dr.', 'NNP'),
('Goldberg', 'NNP'),
('is', 'VBZ'),
('moving', 'VBG'),
('to', 'TO'),
('Arizona', 'NNP'),
('to', 'TO'),
('take', 'VB'),
('a', 'DT'),
('new', 'JJ'),
('position', 'NN'),
```

```
('there', 'RB'),
('in', 'IN'),
('June', 'NNP'),
('He', 'PRP'),
('will', 'MD'),
('be', 'VB'),
('missed', 'VBN'),
('very', 'RB'),
('much', 'JJ'),
('I', 'PRP'),
('think', 'VBP'),
('finding', 'VBG'),
('a', 'DT'),
('new', 'JJ'),
('doctor', 'NN'),
('in', 'IN'),
('NYC', 'NNP'),
('that', 'IN'),
('you', 'PRP'),
('actually', 'RB'),
('like', 'IN'),
('might', 'MD'),
('almost', 'RB'),
('be', 'VB'),
('as', 'RB'),
('awful', 'JJ'),
('as', 'IN'),
('trying', 'VBG'),
('to', 'TO'),
('find', 'VB'),
('a', 'DT'),
('date', 'NN')]
```

```
>>> print([np for np in blob_df[4].noun_phrases])
['got', 'goldberg', 'arizona', 'new position', 'june', 'new doctor', 'nyc']
```

You can see that the noun phrases found by each library are a little bit different. spaCy includes common words in the English language like "a" and "the," while TextBlob removes these. This reflects a difference in the rules engines that drive what each library considers to be a noun phrase. You can also write your part-of-speech relationships to define the chunks you are seeking. See Bird et al. (2009) to really dive deep into chunking with Python from scratch.

Summary

The bag-of-words representation is simple to understand, easy to compute, and useful for classification and search tasks. But sometimes single words are too simplistic to encapsulate some information in the text. To fix this problem, people look to longer sequences. Bag-of-n-grams is a natural generalization of bag-of-words. The concept is still easy to understand, and it's just as easy to compute as bag-of-words.

Bag-of-n-grams generates a lot more distinct n-grams. It increases the feature storage cost, as well as the computation cost of the model training and prediction stages. The number of data points remains the same, but the dimension of the feature space is now much larger. Hence, the data is much more sparse. The higher n is, the higher the storage and computation cost, and the sparser the data. For these reasons, longer n-grams do not always lead to improvements in model accuracy (or any other performance measure). People usually stop at $n = 2$ or 3. Longer n-grams are rarely used.

One way to combat the increase in sparsity and cost is to filter the n-grams and retain only the most meaningful phrases. This is the goal of collocation extraction. In theory, collocations (or phrases) could form nonconsecutive token sequences in the text. In practice, however, looking for nonconsecutive phrases has a much higher computation cost for not much gain. So, collocation extraction usually starts with a candidate list of bigrams and utilizes statistical methods to filter them.

All of these methods turn a sequence of text tokens into a disconnected set of counts. Sets have much less structure than sequences; they lead to flat feature vectors.

In this chapter, we dipped our toes into the water with simple text featurization techniques. These techniques turn a piece of natural language text—full of rich semantic structure—into a simple flat vector. We discussed a number of common filtering techniques to clean up the vector entries. We also introduced n-grams and collocation extraction as methods that add a little more structure into the flat vectors. The next chapter goes into a lot more detail about another common text featurization trick called *tf-idf*. Subsequent chapters will discuss more methods for adding structure back into a flat vector.

Bibliography

Bird, Steven, Ewan Klein, and Edward Loper. *Natural Language Processing with Python.* Sebastopol, CA: O'Reilly Media, 2009.

Dunning, Ted. "Accurate Methods for the Statistics of Surprise and Coincidence." *ACM Journal of Computational Linguistics, special issue on using large corpora* 19:1 (1993): 61–74.

Khan Academy. "Hypothesis Testing and p-Values." Retrieved from *https:// www.khanacademy.org/math/probability/statistics-inferential/hypothesis-testing/v/ hypothesis-testing-and-p-values.*

Manning, Christopher D. and Hinrich Schütze. *Foundations of Statistical Natural Language Processing.* Cambridge, MA: MIT Press, 1999.

## CHAPTER 4

The Effects of Feature Scaling: From Bag-of-Words to Tf-Idf

A bag-of-words representation is simple to generate but far from perfect. If we count all words equally, then some words end up being emphasized more than we need. Recall our example of Emma and the raven from Chapter 3. We'd like a document representation that emphasizes the two main characters. The words "Emma" and "raven" both appear three times, but "the" appears a whopping eight times, "and" appears five times, and "it" and "was" both appear four times. The main characters do not stand out by simple frequency count alone. This is problematic.

It would also be nice to pick out words such as "magnificently," "gleamed," "intimidated," "tentatively," and "reigned," because they help to set the overall tone of the paragraph. They indicate sentiment, which can be very valuable information to a data scientist. So, ideally, we'd like a representation that highlights *meaningful* words.

Tf-Idf : A Simple Twist on Bag-of-Words

Tf-idf is a simple twist on the bag-of-words approach. It stands for *term frequency–inverse document frequency*. Instead of looking at the raw counts of each word in each document in a dataset, tf-idf looks at a normalized count where each word count is divided by the number of documents this word appears in. That is:

bow(w, d) = # times word w appears in document d

tf-idf(w, d) = bow(w, d) * N / (# documents in which word w appears)

N is the total number of documents in the dataset. The fraction N / (# documents ...) is what's known as the *inverse document frequency*. If a word appears in many documents, then its inverse document frequency is close to 1. If a word appears in just a few documents, then the inverse document frequency is much higher.

Alternatively, we can take a log transform instead using the raw inverse document frequency. Logarithm turns 1 into 0, and makes large numbers (those much greater than 1) smaller. (More on this later.)

If we define tf-idf as:

$$\text{tf-idf}(w, d) = \text{bow}(w, d) * \log (N \,/\, \# \text{ documents in which word } w \text{ appears})$$

then a word that appears in every single document will be effectively zeroed out, and a word that appears in very few documents will have an even larger count than before.

Let's look at some pictures to understand what it's all about. Figure 4-1 shows a simple example that contains four sentences: "it is a puppy," "it is a cat," "it is a kitten," and "that is a dog and this is a pen." We plot these sentences in the feature space of three words: "puppy," "cat," and "is."

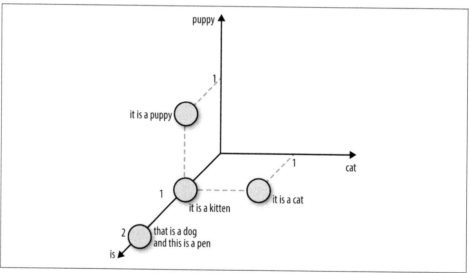

Figure 4-1. Four sentences about dogs and cats

Now let's look at the same four sentences in tf-idf representation using the log transform for the inverse document frequency. Figure 4-2 shows the documents in feature space. Notice that the word "is" is effectively eliminated as a feature since it appears in all sentences in this dataset. Also, because they each appear in only one sentence out of the total four, the words "puppy" and "cat" are now counted higher than before ($\log(4) = 1.38... > 1$). Thus, tf-idf makes rare words more prominent and effectively ignores common words. It is closely related to the frequency-based filtering methods in Chapter 3, but much more mathematically elegant than placing hard cutoff thresholds.

Intuition Behind Tf-Idf

Tf-idf makes rare words more prominent and effectively ignores common words.

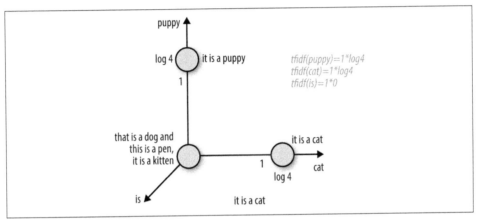

Figure 4-2. Tf-idf representation of the sentences in Figure 4-1

Putting It to the Test

Tf-idf transforms word count features through multiplication with a constant. Hence, it is an example of *feature scaling*, a concept introduced in Chapter 2. How well does feature scaling work in practice? Let's compare the performance of scaled and unscaled features in a simple text classification task. Time for some code!

In Example 4-1, we revisit the Yelp reviews dataset (*http://www.yelp.com/data set_challenge*). Round 6 of the Yelp dataset challenge contains close to 1.6 million reviews of businesses in six US cities.

Example 4-1. Loading and cleaning the Yelp reviews dataset in Python

```
>>> import json
>>> import pandas as pd

# Load Yelp business data
>>> biz_f = open('yelp_academic_dataset_business.json')
>>> biz_df = pd.DataFrame([json.loads(x) for x in biz_f.readlines()])
>>> biz_f.close()
```

```
# Load Yelp reviews data
>>> review_file = open('yelp_academic_dataset_review.json')
>>> review_df = pd.DataFrame([json.loads(x) for x in review_file.readlines()])
>>> review_file.close()

# Pull out only Nightlife and Restaurants businesses
>>> two_biz = biz_df[biz_df.apply(lambda x: 'Nightlife' in x['categories'] or
...                                          'Restaurants' in x['categories'],
...                                axis=1)]

# Join with the reviews to get all reviews on the two types of business
>>> twobiz_reviews = two_biz.merge(review_df, on='business_id', how='inner')

# Trim away the features we won't use
>>> twobiz_reviews = twobiz_reviews[['business_id',
...                                  'name',
...                                  'stars_y',
...                                  'text',
...                                  'categories']]

# Create the target column--True for Nightlife businesses, and False otherwise
>>> two_biz_reviews['target'] = \
...     twobiz_reviews.apply(lambda x: 'Nightlife' in x['categories'],
...                          axis=1)
```

Creating a Classification Dataset

Let's see whether we can use the reviews to categorize a business as either a restaurant or a nightlife venue. To save on training time, we can take a subset of the reviews. In this case, there is a large difference in review count between the two categories. This is called a *class-imbalanced dataset*. Imbalanced datasets are problematic for modeling because the model will expend most of its effort fitting to the larger class. Since we have plenty of data in both classes, a good way to resolve the problem is to down-sample the larger class (restaurants) to be roughly the same size as the smaller class (nightlife). Here is an example workflow:

1. Take a random sample of 10% of nightlife reviews and 2.1% of restaurant reviews (percentages chosen so the number of examples in each class is roughly equal).

2. Create a 70/30 train-test split of this dataset. In this example, the training set ends up with 29,264 reviews, and the test set with 12,542 reviews.

3. The training data contains 46,924 unique words; this is the number of features in the bag-of-words representation.

Example 4-2 shows how we do this.

Example 4-2. Creating a balanced classification dataset

```
# Create a class-balanced subsample to play with
>>> nightlife = \
...    twobiz_reviews[twobiz_reviews.apply(lambda x: 'Nightlife' in x['categories'],
...                               axis=1)]
>>> restaurants = \
...    twobiz_reviews[twobiz_reviews.apply(lambda x: 'Restaurants' in x['categories'],
...                               axis=1)]
>>> nightlife_subset = nightlife.sample(frac=0.1, random_state=123)
>>> restaurant_subset = restaurants.sample(frac=0.021, random_state=123)
>>> combined = pd.concat([nightlife_subset, restaurant_subset])

# Split into training and test datasets
>>> training_data, test_data = modsel.train_test_split(combined,
...                                         train_size=0.7,
...                                         random_state=123)
>>> training_data.shape
(29264, 5)
>>> test_data.shape
(12542, 5)
```

Scaling Bag-of-Words with Tf-Idf Transformation

The goal of this experiment is to compare the effectiveness of bag-of-words, tf-idf, and ℓ^2 normalization for linear classification. Note that doing tf-idf then ℓ^2 normalization is the same as doing ℓ^2 normalization alone. So, we only need to test three sets of features: bag-of-words, tf-idf, and word-wise ℓ^2 normalization on top of bag-of-words.

In Example 4-3, we use scikit-learn's `CountVectorizer` to convert the review text into a bag-of-words. All text featurization methods implicitly depend on a tokenizer, which is the module that converts a text string into a list of tokens (words). In this example, scikit-learn's default tokenizing pattern looks for sequences of two or more alphanumeric characters. Punctuation marks are treated as token separators.

Example 4-3. Transform features

```
# Represent the review text as a bag-of-words
>>> bow_transform = text.CountVectorizer()
>>> X_tr_bow = bow_transform.fit_transform(training_data['text'])
>>> X_te_bow = bow_transform.transform(test_data['text'])
>>> len(bow_transform.vocabulary_)
46924

>>> y_tr = training_data['target']
>>> y_te = test_data['target']

# Create the tf-idf representation using the bag-of-words matrix
```

```
>>> tfidf_trfm = text.TfidfTransformer(norm=None)
>>> X_tr_tfidf = tfidf_trfm.fit_transform(X_tr_bow)
>>> X_te_tfidf = tfidf_trfm.transform(X_te_bow)

# Just for kicks, l2-normalize the bag-of-words representation
>>> X_tr_l2 = preproc.normalize(X_tr_bow, axis=0)
>>> X_te_l2 = preproc.normalize(X_te_bow, axis=0)
```

Feature Scaling on the Test Set

A subtle point about feature scaling is that it requires knowing feature statistics that we most likely do not know in practice, such as the mean, variance, document frequency, ℓ^2 norm, etc. In order to compute the tf-idf representation, we have to compute the inverse document frequencies based on the *training* data and use these statistics to scale both the training and test data. In scikit-learn, fitting the feature transformer on the training data amounts to collecting the relevant statistics. The fitted transformer can then be applied to the test data.

When we use training statistics to scale test data, the result will look a little fuzzy. Min-max scaling on the test set no longer neatly maps to 0 and 1. ℓ^2 norms, mean, and variance statistics will all look a little off. This is less problematic than missing data. For instance, the test set may contain words that are not present in the training data, and we would have no document frequency to use for the new words. The common solution is to simply drop the new words in the test set. This may seem irresponsible, but the model—trained on the training set—would not know what to do with these words anyway. A slightly less hacky option would be to explicitly learn a "garbage" word and map all low-frequency words to it, even within the training set, as discussed in "Rare words" on page 49.

Classification with Logistic Regression

Logistic regression is a simple, linear classifier. Due to its simplicity, it's often a good first classifier to try. It takes a weighted combination of the input features, and passes it through a *sigmoid function*, which smoothly maps any real number to a number between 0 and 1. The function transforms a real number input, x, into a number between 0 and 1. It has one set of parameters, w, which represents the slope of the increase around the midpoint, 0.5. The intercept term b denotes the input value where the function output crosses the midpoint. A logistic classifier would predict the positive class if the sigmoid output is greater than 0.5, and the negative class otherwise. By varying w and b, one can control where that change in decision occurs, and how fast the decision should respond to changing input values around that point.

Figure 4-3 illustrates the sigmoid function.

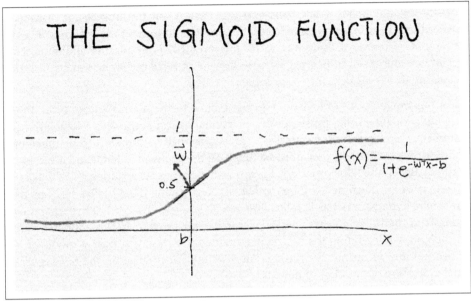

Figure 4-3. Illustration of a sigmoid function

Now let's build some simple logistic regression classifiers on our various feature sets and see how they do (Example 4-4).

Example 4-4. Training logistic regression classifiers with default parameters

```
>>> def simple_logistic_classify(X_tr, y_tr, X_test, y_test, description):
...     ### Helper function to train a logistic classifier and score on test data
...     m = LogisticRegression().fit(X_tr, y_tr)
...     s = m.score(X_test, y_test)
...     print ('Test score with', description, 'features:', s)
...     return m

>>> m1 = simple_logistic_classify(X_tr_bow, y_tr, X_te_bow, y_te, 'bow')
>>> m2 = simple_logistic_classify(X_tr_l2, y_tr, X_te_l2, y_te, 'l2-normalized')
>>> m3 = simple_logistic_classify(X_tr_tfidf, y_tr, X_te_tfidf, y_te, 'tf-idf')
Test score with bow features: 0.775873066497
Test score with l2-normalized features: 0.763514590974
Test score with tf-idf features: 0.743182905438
```

Paradoxically, the results show that the most accurate classifier is the one using BoW features. This was unexpected. As it turns out, the reason is that the classifiers are not well "tuned," which is a common pitfall when comparing classifiers.

Tuning Logistic Regression with Regularization

Logistic regression has a few bells and whistles. When the number of features is greater than the number of data points, the problem of finding the best model is said to be *underdetermined*. One way to fix this problem is by placing additional constraints on the training process. This is known as *regularization*, and its technical details are discussed here.

Most implementations of logistic regression allow for regularization. In order to use this functionality, one must specify a regularization parameter. Regularization parameters are *hyperparameters* that are not learned automatically in the model training process. Rather, they must be tuned on the problem at hand and given to the training algorithm. This process is known as hyperparameter tuning. (For details on how to evaluate machine learning models, see, e.g., Zheng [2015].) One basic method for tuning hyperparameters is called *grid search*: you specify a grid of hyperparameter values and the tuner programmatically searches for the best hyperparameter setting in the grid. After finding the best hyperparameter setting, you train a model on the entire training set using that setting, and use its performance on the test set as the final evaluation of this class of models.

Important: Tune Hyperparameters When Comparing Models

It's essential to tune hyperparameters when comparing models or features. The default settings of a software package will always return a model. But unless the software performs automatic tuning under the hood, it is likely to return a suboptimal model based on suboptimal hyperparameter settings. The sensitivity of classifier performance to hyperparameter settings depends on the model and the distribution of training data. Logistic regression is relatively robust (or insensitive) to hyperparameter settings. Even so, it is necessary to find and use the right *range* of hyperparameters. Otherwise, the advantages of one model versus another may be solely due to tuning parameters, and will not reflect the actual behavior of the model or features.

Even the best autotuning packages still require specifying the upper and lower limits of search, and finding those limits can take a few manual tries.

In the following example, we manually set the search grid of the logistic regularization parameter to {1e-5, 0.001, 0.1, 1, 10, 100}. The upper and lower bounds took a couple of tries to narrow down. The optimal hyperparameter settings for each feature set are given in Table 4-1.

Table 4-1. Best hyperparameter settings for logistic regression on a sample of Yelp reviews of nightlife venues and restaurants

	ℓ^2 regularization
BoW	0.1
ℓ^2-normalized	10
Tf-idf	0.001

We also want to test whether the difference in accuracy between tf-idf and BoW is due to noise. To this end, we use *k*-fold cross validation to simulate having multiple statistically independent datasets. It divides the dataset into *k* folds. The cross validation process iterates through the folds, using all but one fold for training, and validating the results on the fold that is held out.

Estimating Variance via Resampling

Modern statistical methods assume that the underlying data comes from a random distribution. The performance measurements of models derived from data are also subject to random noise. In this situation, it is always a good idea to take the measurement not just once, but multiple times, based on datasets of comparable statistics. This gives us a confidence interval for the measurement.

k-fold cross validation is one such strategy. Resampling is another technique that generates multiple small samples from the same underlying dataset. See Zheng (2015) for more details on resampling.

The GridSearchCV function in scikit-learn runs a grid search with cross validation (see Example 4-5). Figure 4-4 shows a box-and-whiskers plot of the distribution of accuracy measurements for models trained on each of the feature sets. The middle line in the box marks the median accuracy, the box itself marks the region between the first and third quartiles, and the whiskers extend to the rest of the distribution.

Example 4-5. Tuning logistic regression hyperparameters with grid search

```
>>> import sklearn.model_selection as modsel

# Specify a search grid, then do a 5-fold grid search for each of the feature sets
>>> param_grid_ = {'C': [1e-5, 1e-3, 1e-1, 1e0, 1e1, 1e2]}

# Tune classifier for bag-of-words representation
>>> bow_search = modsel.GridSearchCV(LogisticRegression(), cv=5,
...                                   param_grid=param_grid_)
>>> bow_search.fit(X_tr_bow, y_tr)

# Tune classifier for L2-normalized word vector
```

```
>>> l2_search = modsel.GridSearchCV(LogisticRegression(), cv=5,
...                                 param_grid=param_grid_)
>>> l2_search.fit(X_tr_l2, y_tr)

# Tune classifier for tf-idf
>>> tfidf_search = modsel.GridSearchCV(LogisticRegression(), cv=5,
...                                    param_grid=param_grid_)
>>> tfidf_search.fit(X_tr_tfidf, y_tr)

# Let's check out one of the grid search outputs to see how it went
>>> bow_search.cv_results_
{'mean_fit_time': array([ 0.43648252,  0.94630651,
         5.64090128, 15.31248307, 31.47010217, 42.44257565]),
 'mean_score_time': array([ 0.00080056, 0.00392466, 0.00864897, 0 .00784755,
         0.01192751, 0.0072515 ]),
 'mean_test_score': array([ 0.57897075, 0.7518111 , 0.78283898, 0.77381766,
         0.75515992, 0.73937261]),
 'mean_train_score': array([ 0.5792185 , 0.76731652, 0.87697341, 0.94629064,
         0.98357195, 0.99441294]),
 'param_C': masked_array(data = [1e-05 0.001 0.1 1.0 10.0 100.0],
             mask = [False False False False False False],
        fill_value = ?),
 'params': ({'C': 1e-05},
  {'C': 0.001},
  {'C': 0.1},
  {'C': 1.0},
  {'C': 10.0},
  {'C': 100.0}),
 'rank_test_score': array([6, 4, 1, 2, 3, 5]),
 'split0_test_score': array([ 0.58028698, 0.75025624, 0.7799795 , 0.7726341 ,
         0.75247694, 0.74086095]),
 'split0_train_score': array([ 0.57923964, 0.76860316, 0.87560871, 0.94434003,
         0.9819308 , 0.99470312]),
 'split1_test_score': array([ 0.5786776 , 0.74628396, 0.77669571, 0.76627371,
         0 .74867589, 0.73176149]),
 'split1_train_score': array([ 0.57917218, 0.7684849 , 0.87945837, 0.94822946,
         0.98504976, 0.99538678]),
 'split2_test_score': array([ 0.57816504, 0.75533914, 0.78472578, 0.76832394,
         0.74799248, 0.7356911 ]),
 'split2_train_score': array([ 0.57977019, 0.76613558, 0.87689548, 0.94566657,
         0.98368288, 0.99397719]),
 'split3_test_score': array([ 0.57894737, 0.75051265, 0.78332194, 0.77682843,
         0.75768968, 0.73855092]),
 'split3_train_score': array([ 0.57914745, 0.76678626, 0.87634546, 0.94558346,
         0.98385443, 0.99474628]),
 'split4_test_score': array([ 0.57877649, 0.75666439, 0.78947368, 0.78503076,
         0.76896787, 0.75        ]),
 'split4_train_score': array([ 0.57876303, 0.7665727 , 0.87655903, 0.94763369,
         0.98334188, 0.99325132]),
 'std_fit_time': array([ 0.03874582, 0.02297261, 1.18862097, 1.83901079,
         4.21516797, 2.93444269]),
 'std_score_time': array([ 0.00160112, 0.00605009, 0.00623053, 0.00698687,
```

```
        0.00713112,  0.00570195]),
'std_test_score': array([ 0.00070799,  0.00375907,  0.00432957,  0.00668246,
        0.00612049]),
'std_train_score': array([ 0.00032232,  0.00102466,  0.00131222,  0.00143229,
        0.00100223,  0.00073252])}

# Plot the cross validation results in a box-and-whiskers plot to
# visualize and compare classifier performance
>>> search_results = pd.DataFrame.from_dict({
                                'bow': bow_search.cv_results_['mean_test_score'],
...                             'tfidf': tfidf_search.cv_results_['mean_test_score'],
...                             'l2': l2_search.cv_results_['mean_test_score']
...
...                         })

# Our usual matplotlib incantations. Seaborn is used here to make
# the plot pretty.
>>> import matplotlib.pyplot as plt
>>> import seaborn as sns
>>> sns.set_style("whitegrid")

>>> ax = sns.boxplot(data=search_results, width=0.4)
>>> ax.set_ylabel('Accuracy', size=14)
>>> ax.tick_params(labelsize=14)
```

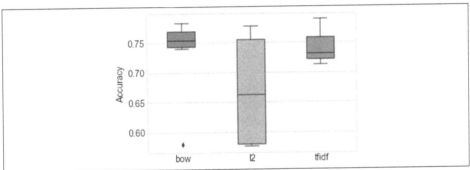

Figure 4-4. Distribution of classifier accuracy under each feature set and regularization setting—the accuracy is measured as the average accuracy from 5-fold cross validation

Table 4-2 shows the average cross validation classifier accuracy for each hyperparameter setting. The asterisk in each column denotes the highest achieved accuracy for that feature set.

Table 4-2. Average cross validation classifier accuracy scores

Regularization parameter	BoW	ℓ^2-normalized	Tf-idf
0.00001	0.578971	0.575724	0.721638
0.001	0.751811	0.575724	0.788648 *
0.1	0.782839 *	0.589120	0.763566
1	0.773818	0.734247	0.741150

Regularization parameter	BoW	ℓ^2-normalized	Tf-idf
10	0.755160	0.776756 *	0.721467
100	0.739373	0.761106	0.712309

The result for ℓ^2 normalized features looks alarmingly bad in Figure 4-4. But don't be fooled. The low accuracy numbers are due to very bad regularization parameter settings—concrete proof that suboptimal hyperparameters can lead to very wrong conclusions. If we train a model using the best hyperparameter setting for each feature set, as in Example 4-6, the accuracy scores of the different feature sets are very close.

Example 4-6. Final training and testing step to compare the different feature sets

```
# Train a final model on the entire training set, using the best hyperparameter
# settings found previously. Measure accuracy on the test set.
>>> m1 = simple_logistic_classify(X_tr_bow, y_tr, X_te_bow, y_te, 'bow',
...                               _C=bow_search.best_params_['C'])
>>> m2 = simple_logistic_classify(X_tr_l2, y_tr, X_te_l2, y_te, 'l2-normalized',
...                               _C=l2_search.best_params_['C'])
>>> m3 = simple_logistic_classify(X_tr_tfidf, y_tr, X_te_tfidf, y_te, 'tf-idf',
...                               _C=tfidf_search.best_params_['C'])
Test score with bow features: 0.78360708021
Test score with l2-normalized features: 0.780178599904
Test score with tf-idf features: 0.788470738319
```

Proper tuning improved the accuracy of all the feature sets, and all three now yield similar classification accuracy under regularized logistic regression. The accuracy score for the tf-idf model is slightly higher, but the difference is likely not statistically significant. These results are completely mystifying. If feature scaling doesn't work better than vanilla bag-of-words, then why do it at all? Why all the hoopla if tf-idf doesn't do anything? We'll explore the answers to those questions in the next section.

Deep Dive: What Is Happening?

In order to understand the "why" behind the results, we have to look at how the features are being used by the model. For linear models like logistic regression, this happens through an intermediary object called the *data matrix*.

The data matrix contains data points represented as fixed-length flat vectors. With bag-of-words vectors, the data matrix is also known as the *document-term matrix*. Figure 3-1 shows a bag-of-words vector in vector form, and Figure 4-1 illustrates four bag-of-words vectors in feature space. To form a document-term matrix, simply take the document vectors, lay them out flat, and stack them on top of one another. The columns represent all possible words in the vocabulary (see Figure 4-5). Since most documents contain only a small subset of all possible words, most of the entries in this matrix are zeros; it is a *sparse* matrix.

	it	is	puppy	cat	pen	a	this
it is a puppy	1	1	1	0	0	1	0
it is a kitten	1	1	0	0	0	1	0
it is a cat	1	1	0	1	0	1	0
that is a dog and this is a pen	0	2	0	0	1	2	1
it is a matrix	1	1	0	0	0	1	0

Figure 4-5. An example document-term matrix of five documents and seven words

Feature scaling methods are essentially column operations on the data matrix. In particular, tf-idf and ℓ^2 normalization both multiply the entire column (an *n*-gram feature, for example) by a constant.

Tf-Idf = Column Scaling

Tf-idf and ℓ^2 normalization are both column operations on the data matrix.

As discussed in Appendix A, training a linear classifier boils down to finding the best linear combination of features, which are column vectors of the data matrix. The solution space is characterized by the column space and the null space of the data matrix. The quality of the trained linear classifier directly depends upon the null space and the column space of the data matrix. A large column space means that there is little linear dependency between the features, which is generally good. The null space contains "novel" data points that cannot be formulated as linear combinations of existing data; a large null space could be problematic. (A perusal of Appendix A is highly recommended for readers who would appreciate a review on concepts such as the linear decision surface, eigen decomposition, and the fundamental subspaces of a matrix.)

How do column scaling operations affect the column space and null space of the data matrix? The answer is "Not very much." But there is a small chance that tf-idf and ℓ^2 normalization could be different. We'll look at why now.

The null space of the data matrix can be large for a couple of reasons. First, many datasets contain data points that are very similar to one another. This means the effective row space is small compared to the number of data points in the dataset. Second, the number of features can be much larger than the number of data points. Bag-of-words is particularly good at creating giant feature spaces. In our Yelp example, there are 47K features in 29K reviews in the training set. Moreover, the number of distinct words usually grows with the number of documents in the dataset, so adding more documents would not necessarily decrease the feature-to-data ratio or reduce the null space.

With bag-of-words, the column space is relatively small compared to the number of features. There could be words that appear roughly the same number of times in the same documents. This would lead to the corresponding column vectors being nearly linearly dependent, which leads to the column space being not as full rank as it could be (see Appendix A for the definition of full rank). This is called a *rank deficiency*. (Much like how animals can be deficient in vitamins and minerals, matrices can be deficient in rank, and the output space will not be as fluffy as it should.)

Rank-deficient row space and column space lead to the model being overly provisioned for the problem. The linear model outfits a weight parameter for each feature in the dataset. If the row and column spaces were full rank,[1] then the model would allow us to generate any target vector in the output space. When they are rank deficient, the model has more degrees of freedom than it needs. This makes it harder to pin down a solution.

Can feature scaling solve the rank deficiency problem of the data matrix? Let's take a look.

The column space is defined as the linear combination of all column vectors (boldface indicates a vector): $a_1\mathbf{v}_1 + a_2\mathbf{v}_2 + ... + a_n\mathbf{v}_n$. Feature scaling replaces a column vector with a constant multiple, say $\mathbf{v}_1 = c\mathbf{v}_1$. But we can still generate the original linear combination by just replacing a_1 with $\breve{a}_1 = a_1 / c$. It appears that feature scaling does not change the rank of the column space. Similarly, feature scaling does not affect the rank of the null space, because one can counteract the scaled feature column by reverse scaling the corresponding entry in the weight vector.

However, as usual, there is one catch. If the scalar is 0, then there is no way to recover the original linear combination; $\mathbf{v}_1$ is gone. If that vector is linearly independent from all the other columns, then we've effectively shrunk the column space and enlarged the null space.

If that vector is not correlated with the target output, then this is effectively pruning away noisy signals, which is a good thing. This turns out to be the key difference between tf-idf and ℓ^2 normalization. ℓ^2 normalization would never compute a norm of zero, unless the vector contains all zeros. If the vector is close to zero, then its norm is also close to zero. Dividing by the small norm would accentuate the vector and make it longer.

---

1 Strictly speaking, the row space and column space for a rectangular matrix cannot both be full rank. The maximum rank for both subspaces is the smaller of m (the number of rows) and n (the number of columns).

Tf-idf, on the other hand, can generate scaling factors that are close to zero, as shown in Figure 4-2. This happens when the word is present in a large number of documents in the training set. Such a word is likely not strongly correlated with the target vector. Pruning it away allows the solver to focus on the other directions in the column space and find better solutions (although the improvement in accuracy will probably not be huge, because there are typically few noisy directions that are prunable in this way).

Where feature scaling—both ℓ^2 and tf-idf—does have a telling effect is on the convergence speed of the solver. This is a sign that the data matrix now has a much smaller condition number (the ratio between the largest and smallest singular values—see Appendix A for a full discussion of these terms). In fact, ℓ^2 normalization makes the condition number nearly 1. But it's not the case that the better the condition number, the better the solution. During this experiment, ℓ^2 normalization converged much faster than either BoW or tf-idf. But it is also more sensitive to overfitting: it requires much more regularization and is more sensitive to the number of iterations during optimization.

Summary

In this chapter, we used tf-idf as an entry point into a detailed analysis of how feature transformations can affect the model (or not). Tf-idf is an example of feature scaling, so we contrasted its performance with that of another feature scaling method—ℓ^2 normalization.

The results were not as one might have expected. Tf-idf and ℓ^2 normalization do not improve the final classifier's accuracy above plain bag-of-words. After acquiring some statistical modeling and linear algebra chops, we realize why: neither of them changes the column space of the data matrix.

One small difference between the two is that tf-idf can "stretch" the word count as well as "compress" it. In other words, it makes some counts bigger, and others close to zero. Therefore, tf-idf could altogether eliminate uninformative words.

Along the way, we also discovered another effect of feature scaling: it improves the condition number of the data matrix, making linear models much faster to train. Both ℓ^2 normalization and tf-idf have this effect.

To summarize, the lesson is: the *right* feature scaling can be helpful for classification. The right scaling accentuates the informative words and downweights the common words. It can also improve the condition number of the data matrix. The right scaling is not necessarily uniform column scaling.

This story is a wonderful illustration of the difficulty of analyzing the effects of feature engineering in the general case. Changing the features affects the training process and the models that ensue. Linear models are the simplest models to understand, yet it still takes very careful experimentation methodology and a lot of deep mathematical knowledge to tease apart the theoretical and practical impacts. This would be mostly impossible with more complicated models or feature transformations.

Bibliography

Zheng, Alice. *Evaluating Machine Learning Models.* Sebastopol, CA: O'Reilly Media, 2015.

## CHAPTER 5

Categorical Variables: Counting Eggs in the Age of Robotic Chickens

A *categorical variable*, as the name suggests, is used to represent categories or labels. For instance, a categorical variable could represent major cities in the world, the four seasons in a year, or the industry (oil, travel, technology) of a company. The number of category values is always finite in a real-world dataset. The values may be represented numerically. However, unlike other numeric variables, the values of a categorical variable cannot be ordered with respect to one another. (*Oil* is neither greater than nor less than *travel* as an industry type.) They are called *nonordinal*.

A simple question can serve as litmus test for whether something should be a categorical variable: "Does it matter *how* different two values are, or only that they *are* different?" A stock price of $500 is five times higher than a price of $100. So, stock price should be represented by a continuous numeric variable. The industry of the company (oil, travel, tech, etc.), on the other hand, should probably be categorical.

Large categorical variables are particularly common in transactional records. For instance, many web services track users using an ID, which is a categorical variable with hundreds to hundreds of millions of values, depending on the number of unique users of the service. The IP address of an internet transaction is another example of a large categorical variable. They are categorical variables because, even though user IDs and IP addresses are numeric, their magnitude is usually not relevant to the task at hand. For instance, the IP address might be relevant when doing fraud detection on individual transactions—some IP addresses or subnets may generate more fraudulent transactions than others. But a subnet of 164.203.x.x is not inherently more fraudulent than 164.202.x.x; the numeric value of the subnet does not matter.

The vocabulary of a document corpus can be interpreted as a large categorical variable, with the categories being unique words. It can be computationally expensive to represent so many distinct categories. If a category (e.g., word) appears multiple times in a data point (document), then we can represent it as a count, and represent all of the categories through their count statistics. This is called *bin counting*. We start this discussion with common representations of categorical variables, and eventually meander our way to a discussion of bin counting for large categorical variables, which are very common in modern datasets.

Encoding Categorical Variables

The categories of a categorical variable are usually not numeric.[1] For example, eye color can be "black," "blue," "brown," etc. Thus, an encoding method is needed to turn these nonnumeric categories into numbers. It is tempting to simply assign an integer, say from 1 to k, to each of k possible categories—but the resulting values would be orderable against each other, which should not be permissible for categories. So, let's look at some alternatives.

One-Hot Encoding

A better method is to use a group of bits. Each bit represents a possible category. If the variable cannot belong to multiple categories at once, then only one bit in the group can be "on." This is called *one-hot encoding*, and it is implemented in scikit-learn as sklearn.preprocessing.OneHotEncoder (*http://bit.ly/2tmlzTn*). Each of the bits is a feature. Thus, a categorical variable with k possible categories is encoded as a feature vector of length k. Table 5-1 shows an example.

Table 5-1. One-hot encoding of a category of three cities

	e_1	e_2	e_3
San Francisco	1	0	0
New York	0	1	0
Seattle	0	0	1

One-hot encoding is very simple to understand, but it uses one more bit than is strictly necessary. If we see that $k-1$ of the bits are 0, then the last bit must be 1 because the variable must take on one of the k values. Mathematically, one can write this constraint as "the sum of all bits must be equal to 1":

$$e_1 + e_2 + ... + e_k = 1$$

---

[1] In standard statistics literature, the technical term for the categories is *levels*. A categorical variable with two distinct categories has two levels. But there are a number of other things in statistics that are also called levels, so we do not use that terminology here; instead we use the more colloquial and unambiguous term "categories."

Thus, we have a linear dependency on our hands. Linear dependent features, as we discovered in Chapter 4, are slightly annoying because they mean that the trained linear models will not be unique. Different linear combinations of the features can make the same predictions, so we would need to jump through extra hoops to understand the effect of a feature on the prediction.

Dummy Coding

The problem with one-hot encoding is that it allows for k degrees of freedom, while the variable itself needs only $k-1$. *Dummy coding*[2] removes the extra degree of freedom by using only $k-1$ features in the representation (see Table 5-2). One feature is thrown under the bus and represented by the vector of all zeros. This is known as the *reference category*. Dummy coding and one-hot encoding are both implemented in Pandas as `pandas.get_dummies` (*http://bit.ly/2mBNeJx*).

Table 5-2. Dummy coding of a category of three cities

	e_1	e_2
San Francisco	1	0
New York	0	1
Seattle	0	0

The outcome of modeling with dummy coding is more interpretable than with one-hot encoding. This is easy to see in a simple linear regression problem. Suppose we have some data about apartment rental prices in three cities: San Francisco, New York, and Seattle (see Table 5-3).

Table 5-3. Toy dataset of apartment prices in three cities

	City	Rent
0	SF	3999
1	SF	4000
2	SF	4001
3	NYC	3499
4	NYC	3500
5	NYC	3501
6	Seattle	2499

---

2 Curious readers might wonder why one is called coding and the other encoding. This is largely convention. My guess is that one-hot encoding first became popular in electrical engineering, where information is encoded and decoded all the time. Dummy coding and effect coding, on the other hand, were invented in the statistics community. Somehow the "en" didn't make its way over the academic divide.

	City	Rent
7	Seattle	2500
8	Seattle	2501

We can train a linear regressor to predict rental price based solely on the identity of the city (see Example 5-1).

The linear regression model can be written as:

$$y = w_1 x_1 + \dots + w_n x_n$$

It is customary to fit an extra constant term called the *intercept*, so that y can be a nonzero value when the x's are zeros:

$$y = w_1 x_1 + \dots + w_n x_n + b$$

Example 5-1. Linear regression on a categorical variable using one-hot and dummy codes

```
>>> import pandas
>>> from sklearn import linear_model

# Define a toy dataset of apartment rental prices in
# New York, San Francisco, and Seattle
>>> df = pd.DataFrame({
...     'City': ['SF', 'SF', 'SF', 'NYC', 'NYC', 'NYC',
...              'Seattle', 'Seattle', 'Seattle'],
...     'Rent': [3999, 4000, 4001, 3499, 3500, 3501, 2499, 2500, 2501]
... })
>>> df['Rent'].mean()
3333.3333333333335

# Convert the categorical variables in the DataFrame to one-hot encoding
# and fit a linear regression model
>>> one_hot_df = pd.get_dummies(df, prefix=['city'])
>>> one_hot_df
   Rent  city_NYC  city_SF  city_Seattle
0  3999       0.0      1.0           0.0
1  4000       0.0      1.0           0.0
2  4001       0.0      1.0           0.0
3  3499       1.0      0.0           0.0
4  3500       1.0      0.0           0.0
5  3501       1.0      0.0           0.0
6  2499       0.0      0.0           1.0
7  2500       0.0      0.0           1.0
8  2501       0.0      0.0           1.0

>>> model = linear_regression.LinearRegression()
```

```
>>> model.fit(one_hot_df[['city_NYC', 'city_SF', 'city_Seattle']],
...            one_hot_df['Rent'])
>>> model.coef_
array([ 166.66666667,  666.66666667, -833.33333333])
>>> model.intercept_
3333.3333333333335

# Train a linear regression model on dummy code
# Specify the 'drop_first' flag to get dummy coding
>>> dummy_df = pd.get_dummies(df, prefix=['city'], drop_first=True)
>>> dummy_df
   Rent  city_SF  city_Seattle
0  3999    1.0        0.0
1  4000    1.0        0.0
2  4001    1.0        0.0
3  3499    0.0        0.0
4  3500    0.0        0.0
5  3501    0.0        0.0
6  2499    0.0        1.0
7  2500    0.0        1.0
8  2501    0.0        1.0

>>> model.fit(dummy_df[['city_SF', 'city_Seattle']], dummy_df['Rent'])
>>> model.coef_
array([  500., -1000.])
>>> model.intercept_
3500.0
```

With one-hot encoding, the intercept term represents the global mean of the target
variable, Rent, and each of the linear coefficients represents how much that city's
average rent differs from the global mean.

With dummy coding, the bias coefficient represents the mean value of the response
variable y for the reference category, which in the example is the city NYC. The coefficient for the ith feature is equal to the difference between the mean response value
for the ith category and the mean of the reference category.

You can see pretty clearly in Table 5-4 how these methods produce very different
coefficients for linear models.

Table 5-4. Linear regression learned coefficients

	x_1	x_2	x_3	b
One-hot encoding	166.67	666.67	−833.33	3333.33
Dummy coding	0	500	−1000	3500

Effect Coding

Yet another variant of categorical variable encoding is *effect coding*. Effect coding is very similar to dummy coding, with the difference that the reference category is now represented by the vector of all −1's.

Table 5-5. Effect coding of a categorical variable representing three cities

	e_1	e_2
San Francisco	1	0
New York	0	1
Seattle	−1	−1

Effect coding is very similar to dummy coding, but results in linear regression models that are even simpler to interpret. Example 5-2 demonstrates what happens with effect coding as input. The intercept term represents the global mean of the target variable, and the individual coefficients indicate how much the means of the individual categories differ from the global mean. (This is called the *main effect* of the category or level, hence the name "effect coding.") One-hot encoding actually came up with the same intercept and coefficients, but in that case there are linear coefficients for each city. In effect coding, no single feature represents the reference category, so the effect of the reference category needs to be separately computed as the negative sum of the coefficients of all other categories. (See *"FAQ: What is effect coding?"* (*http://www.ats.ucla.edu/stat/mult_pkg/faq/general/effect.htm*) on the UCLA IDRE website for more details.)

Example 5-2. Linear regression with effect coding

```
>>> effect_df = dummy_df.copy()
>>> effect_df.ix[3:5, ['city_SF', 'city_Seattle']] = -1.0
>>> effect_df
   Rent  city_SF  city_Seattle
0  3999     1.0           0.0
1  4000     1.0           0.0
2  4001     1.0           0.0
3  3499    -1.0          -1.0
4  3500    -1.0          -1.0
5  3501    -1.0          -1.0
6  2499     0.0           1.0
7  2500     0.0           1.0
8  2501     0.0           1.0

>>> model.fit(effect_df[['city_SF', 'city_Seattle']], effect_df['Rent'])
>>> model.coef_
array([ 666.66666667, -833.33333333])
>>> model.intercept_
3333.3333333333335
```

Pros and Cons of Categorical Variable Encodings

One-hot, dummy, and effect coding are very similar to one another. They each have pros and cons. One-hot encoding is redundant, which allows for multiple valid models for the same problem. The nonuniqueness is sometimes problematic for interpretation, but the advantage is that each feature clearly corresponds to a category. Moreover, missing data can be encoded as the all-zeros vector, and the output should be the overall mean of the target variable.

Dummy coding and effect coding are not redundant. They give rise to unique and interpretable models. The downside of dummy coding is that it cannot easily handle missing data, since the all-zeros vector is already mapped to the reference category. It also encodes the effect of each category relative to the reference category, which may look strange.

Effect coding avoids this problem by using a different code for the reference category, but the vector of all –1's is a dense vector, which is expensive for both storage and computation. For this reason, popular ML software packages such as Pandas and scikit-learn have opted for dummy coding or one-hot encoding instead of effect coding.

All three encoding techniques break down when the number of categories becomes very large. Different strategies are needed to handle extremely large categorical variables.

Dealing with Large Categorical Variables

Automated data collection on the internet can generate large categorical variables. This is common in applications such as targeted advertising and fraud detection.

In targeted advertising, the task is to match a user with a set of ads. Features include the user ID, the website domain for the ad, the search query, the current page, and all possible pairwise conjunctions of those features. (The query is a text string that can be chopped up and turned into the usual text features. However, queries are generally short and are often composed of phrases, so the best course of action in this case is usually to keep them intact, or pass them through a hash function to make storage and comparisons easier. We will discuss hashing in more detail later.) Each of these is a very large categorical variable. The challenge is to find a good feature representation that is memory efficient, yet produces accurate models that are fast to train.

Existing solutions can be categorized (haha) thus:

1. Do nothing fancy with the encoding. Use a simple model that is cheap to train. Feed one-hot encoding into a linear model (logistic regression or linear support vector machine) on lots of machines.

2. Compress the features. There are two choices:
    a. Feature hashing, popular with linear models
    b. Bin counting, popular with linear models as well as trees

Using the vanilla one-hot encoding is a valid option. For Microsoft's search advertising engine, Graepel et al. (2010) report using such binary-valued features in a Bayesian probit regression model that can be trained online using simple updates. Meanwhile, other groups argue for the compression approach. Researchers from Yahoo! swear by feature hashing (Weinberger et al., 2009), though McMahan et al. (2013) experimented with feature hashing on Google's advertising engine and did not find significant improvements. Yet other folks at Microsoft are taken with the idea of bin counting (Bilenko, 2015).

As we shall see, all of these ideas have pros and cons. We will first describe the solutions themselves, then discuss their trade-offs.

Feature Hashing

A *hash function* is a deterministic function that maps a potentially unbounded integer to a finite integer range $[1, m]$. Since the input domain is potentially larger than the output range, multiple numbers may get mapped to the same output. This is called a *collision*. A *uniform hash function* ensures that roughly the same number of numbers are mapped into each of the m bins.

Visually, we can think of a hash function as a machine that intakes numbered balls (keys) and routes them to one of m bins. Balls with the same number will always get routed to the same bin (see Figure 5-1). This maintains the feature space while reducing the storage and processing time during machine learning training and evaluation cycles.

Hash functions can be constructed for any object that can be represented numerically (which is true for any data that can be stored on a computer): numbers, strings, complex structures, etc.

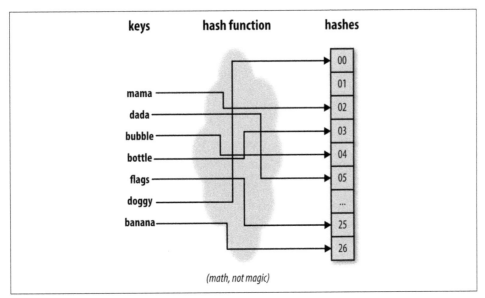

Figure 5-1. Hash functions map keys to bins

When there are very many features, storing the feature vector could take up a lot of space. Feature hashing compresses the original feature vector into an m-dimensional vector by applying a hash function to the feature ID, as shown in Example 5-3. For instance, if the original features were words in a document, then the hashed version would have a fixed vocabulary size of m, no matter how many unique words there are in the input.

Example 5-3. Feature hashing for word features

```
>>> def hash_features(word_list, m):
...     output = [0] * m
...     for word in word_list:
...         index = hash_fcn(word) % m
...         output[index] += 1
...     return output
```

Another variation of feature hashing adds a sign component, so that counts are either added to or subtracted from the hashed bin (see Example 5-4). Statistically speaking, this ensures that the inner products between hashed features are equal in expectation to those of the original features.

Example 5-4. Signed feature hashing

```
>>> def hash_features(word_list, m):
...     output = [0] * m
```

```
...        for word in word_list:
...            index = hash_fcn(word) % m
...            sign_bit = sign_hash(word) % 2
...            if (sign_bit == 0):
...                output[index] -= 1
...            else:
...                output[index] += 1
...        return output
```

The value of the inner product after hashing is within $O\left(\frac{1}{\sqrt{m}}\right)$ of the original inner product, so the size of the hash table m can be selected based on acceptable errors. In practice, picking the right m could take some trial and error.

Feature hashing can be used for models that involve the inner product of feature vectors and coefficients, such as linear models and kernel methods. It has been demonstrated to be successful in the task of spam filtering (Weinberger et al., 2009). In the case of targeted advertising, McMahan et al. (2013) report not being able to get the prediction errors down to an acceptable level unless m is on the order of billions, which does not constitute enough saving in space.

One downside to feature hashing is that the hashed features, being aggregates of original features, are no longer interpretable.

In Example 5-5, we use the Yelp reviews dataset to demonstrate storage and interpretability trade-offs using scikit-learn's `FeatureHasher`.

Example 5-5. Feature hashing (a.k.a. "the hashing trick")

```
>>> import pandas as pd
>>> import json

# Load the first 10,000 reviews
>>> f = open('yelp_academic_dataset_review.json')
>>> js = []
>>> for i in range(10000):
...     js.append(json.loads(f.readline()))
>>> f.close()
>>> review_df = pd.DataFrame(js)

# Define m as equal to the unique number of business_ids
>>> m = len(review_df.business_id.unique())
>>> m
528

>>> from sklearn.feature_extraction import FeatureHasher
>>> h = FeatureHasher(n_features=m, input_type='string')
>>> f = h.transform(review_df['business_id'])

# How does this affect feature interpretability?
```

```
>>> review_df['business_id'].unique().tolist()[0:5]
['vcNAWiLM4dR7D2nwwJ7nCA',
 'UsFtqoBl7naz8AVUBZMjQQ',
 'cE27W9VPg088Qxe4ol6y_g',
 'HZdLhv6COCleJMo7nPl-RA',
 'mVHrayjG3uZ_RLHkLj-AMg']

>>> f.toarray()
array([[ 0.,  0.,  0., ...,  0.,  0.,  0.],
       [ 0.,  0.,  0., ...,  0.,  0.,  0.],
       [ 0.,  0.,  0., ...,  0.,  0.,  0.],
       ...,
       [ 0.,  0.,  0., ...,  0.,  0.,  0.],
       [ 0.,  0.,  0., ...,  0.,  0.,  0.],
       [ 0.,  0.,  0., ...,  0.,  0.,  0.]])

# Not great. BUT, let's see the storage size of our features.
>>> from sys import getsizeof
>>> print('Our pandas Series, in bytes: ', getsizeof(review_df['business_id']))
>>> print('Our hashed numpy array, in bytes: ', getsizeof(f))
Our pandas Series, in bytes:  790104
Our hashed numpy array, in bytes:  56
```

We can clearly see how using feature hashing will benefit us computationally, sacrificing immediate user interpretability. This is an easy trade-off to accept when progressing from data exploration and visualization into a machine learning pipeline for large datasets.

Bin Counting

Bin counting is one of the perennial rediscoveries in machine learning. It has been reinvented and used in a variety of applications, from ad click-through rate prediction to hardware branch prediction (Yeh and Patt, 1991; Lee et al., 1998; Chen et al., 2009; Li et al., 2010). Yet because it is a feature engineering technique and not a modeling or optimization method, there is no research paper on the topic. The most detailed description of the technique can be found in Misha Bilenko's (2015) blog post "Big Learning Made Easy—with Counts!" (*http://bit.ly/2tnICgH*) and the associated slides (*http://bit.ly/2FiuRW6*).

The idea of bin counting is deviously simple: rather than using the *value* of the categorical variable as the feature, instead use the *conditional probability* of the target under that value. In other words, instead of encoding the identity of the categorical value, we compute the association statistics between that value and the target that we wish to predict. For those familiar with naive Bayes classifiers, this statistic should ring a bell, because it is the conditional probability of the class under the assumption that all features are independent. It is best illustrated with an example (see Table 5-6).

Table 5-6. Example of bin-counting features (reproduced from "Big Learning Made Easy—with Counts!" with permission)

User	Number of clicks	Number of nonclicks	Probability of click	QueryHash, AdDomain	Number of clicks	Number of nonclicks	Probability of click
Alice	5	120	0.0400	0x598fd4fe, foo.com	5,000	30,000	0.167
Bob	20	230	0.0800	0x50fa3cc0, bar.org	100	900	0.100
...				...			...
Joe	2	3	0.400	0x437a45e1, qux.net	6	18	0.250

Bin counting assumes that historical data is available for computing the statistics. Table 5-6 contains aggregated historical counts for each possible value of the categorical variables. Based on the number of times the user "Alice" has clicked on any ad and the number of times she has not clicked, we can calculate the probability of her clicking on any ad. Similarly, we can compute the probability of a click for any query–ad domain combination. At training time, every time we see "Alice," we can use her *probability of click* as the input feature to the model. The same goes for QueryHash–AdDomain pairs like "0x437a45e1, qux.net."

Suppose there were 10,000 users. One-hot encoding would generate a sparse vector of length 10,000, with a single 1 in the column that corresponds to the value of the current data point. Bin counting would encode all 10,000 binary columns as a single feature with a real value between 0 and 1.

We can include other features in addition to the historical click-through probability: the raw counts themselves (number of clicks and nonclicks), the log-odds ratio, or any other derivatives of probability. Our example here is for predicting ad click-through rates, but the technique readily applies to general binary classification. It can also be readily extended to multiclass classification using the usual techniques to extend binary classifiers to multiclass; i.e., via one-against-many odds ratios or other multiclass label encodings.

Odds Ratio and Log Odds Ratio for Bin Counting

The odds ratio is usually defined between two binary variables. It looks at their strength of association by asking the question, "How much more likely is it for Y to be true when X is true?" For instance, we might ask, "How much more likely is Alice to click on an ad than the general population?" Here, X is the binary variable "Alice is the current user," and Y is the variable "click on ad or not." The computation uses what's called the two-way contingency table (basically, four numbers that correspond to the four possible combinations of X and Y), as seen in Table 5-7.

Table 5-7. Contingency table for ad click and user

	Click	Nonclick	Total
Alice	5	120	125
Not Alice	995	18,880	19,875
Total	1,000	19,000	20,000

Given an input variable X and a target variable Y, the odds ratio is defined as:

$$\text{odds ratio} = \frac{P(Y = 1 \mid X = 1) / P(Y = 0 \mid X = 1)}{P(Y = 1 \mid X = 0) / P(Y = 0 \mid X = 0)}$$

In our example, this translates as the ratio between "how much more likely is it that Alice clicks on an ad rather than does not click" and "how much more likely is it that other people click rather than not click." The number, in this case, is:

$$\text{odds ratio (user, ad click)} = \frac{(5 / 125) / (120 / 125)}{(995 / 19,875) / (18,880 / 19,875)} = 0.7906$$

More simply, we can just look at the numerator, which examines how much more likely it is that a single user (Alice) clicks on an ad versus not clicking. This is suitable for large categorical variables with many values, not just two:

$$\text{odds ratio (Alice, ad click)} = \frac{5 / 125}{120 / 125} = 0.04166$$

Probability ratios can easily become very small or very large. (For instance, there will be users who almost never click on ads, and perhaps users who click on ads much more frequently than not.) The log transform again comes to our rescue. Another useful property of the logarithm is that it turns a division into a subtraction:

$$\text{log-odds ratio (Alice, ad click)} = log\left(\frac{5}{125}\right) - log\left(\frac{120}{125}\right) = -3.178$$

In short, bin counting converts a categorical variable into statistics about the value. It turns a large, sparse, binary representation of the categorical variable, such as that produced by one-hot encoding, into a very small, dense, real-valued numeric representation (Figure 5-2).

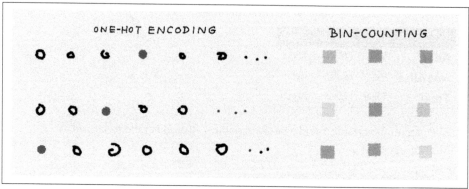

Figure 5-2. An illustration of one-hot encoding versus bin-counting statistics for categorical variables

In terms of implementation, bin counting requires storing a map between each category and its associated counts. (The rest of the statistics can be derived on the fly from the raw counts.) Hence it requires $O(k)$ space, where k is the number of unique values of the categorical variable.

To illustrate bin counting in practice, we'll use data from a Kaggle competition hosted by Avazu (*https://www.kaggle.com/c/avazu-ctr-prediction*). Here are some relevant statistics about the dataset:

- There are 24 variables, including `click`, a binary click/no click counter, and `device_id`, which tracks which device an ad was displayed on.
- The full dataset contains 40,428,967 observations, with 2,686,408 unique devices.

The aim of the Avazu competition was to predict click-through rate using ad data, but we will use the dataset to demonstrate how bin counting can greatly reduce the feature space for large amounts of streaming data (see Example 5-6).

Example 5-6. Bin-counting example

```
>>> import pandas as pd

# train_subset data is first 10K rows of 6+GB set
>>> df = pd.read_csv('data/train_subset.csv')

# How many unique features should we have after?
>>> len(df['device_id'].unique())
7201

# For each category, we want to calculate:
# Theta = [counts, p(click), p(no click), p(click)/p(no click)]

>>> def click_counting(x, bin_column):
```

```
...          clicks = pd.Series(x[x['click'] > 0][bin_column].value_counts(),
...                               name='clicks')
...          no_clicks = pd.Series(x[x['click'] < 1][bin_column].value_counts(),
...                               name='no_clicks')

...          counts = pd.DataFrame([clicks,no_clicks]).T.fillna('0')
...          counts['total_clicks'] = counts['clicks'].astype('int64') +
...                               counts['no_clicks'].astype('int64')
...          return counts

>>> def bin_counting(counts):
...          counts['N+'] = counts['clicks']
...                      .astype('int64')
...                      .divide(counts['total_clicks'].astype('int64'))
...          counts['N-'] = counts['no_clicks']
...                      .astype('int64')
...                      .divide(counts['total_clicks'].astype('int64'))
...          counts['log_N+'] = counts['N+'].divide(counts['N-'])
...          # If we wanted to only return bin-counting properties,
...          # we would filter here
...          bin_counts = counts.filter(items= ['N+', 'N-', 'log_N+'])
...          return counts, bin_counts

# Bin counts example: device_id
>>> bin_column = 'device_id'
>>> device_clicks = click_counting(df.filter(items=[bin_column, 'click']),
...                               bin_column)
>>> device_all, device_bin_counts = bin_counting(device_clicks)

# Check to make sure we have all the devices
>>> len(device_bin_counts)
7201

>>> device_all.sort_values(by = 'total_clicks', ascending=False).head(4)
```

	clicks	no_clicks	total	N+	N-	log_N+
a99f214a	15729	71206	86935	0.180928	0.819072	0.220894
c357dbff	33	134	167	0.197605	0.802395	0.246269
31da1bd0	0	62	62	0.000000	1.000000	0.000000
936e92fb	5	54	59	0.084746	0.915254	0.092593

What about rare categories?

Just like rare words, rare categories require special treatment. Think about a user who logs in once a year: there will be very little data to reliably estimate that user's click-through rate for ads. Moreover, rare categories waste space in the counts table.

One way to deal with this is through *back-off*, a simple technique that accumulates the counts of all rare categories in a special bin (see Figure 5-3). If the count is greater than a certain threshold, then the category gets its own count statistics. Otherwise, we use the statistics from the back-off bin. This essentially reverts the statistics for a single rare category to the statistics computed on all rare categories. When using the back-off method, it helps to also add a binary indicator for whether or not the statistics come from the back-off bin.

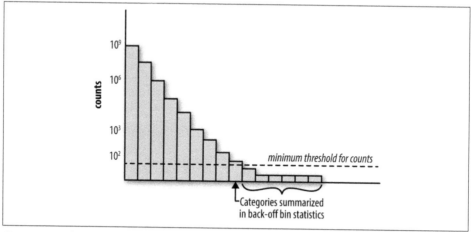

Figure 5-3. If a rare category gains counts, it can move above the threshold for the back-off bin, using its own count statistics for modeling

There is another way to deal with this problem, called the *count-min sketch* (Cormode and Muthukrishnan, 2005). In this method, all the categories, rare or frequent alike, are mapped through multiple hash functions with an output range, m, much smaller than the number of categories, k. When retrieving a statistic, recompute all the hashes of the category and return the smallest statistic. Having multiple hash functions mitigates the probability of collision within a single hash function. The scheme works because the number of hash functions times m, the size of the hash table, can be made smaller than k, the number of categories, and still retain low overall collision probability.

Figure 5-4 illustrates. Each item i is mapped to one cell in each row of the array of counts. When an update of c_t to item i_t arrives, c_t is added to each of these cells, hashed using functions $h_1 \ldots h_d$.

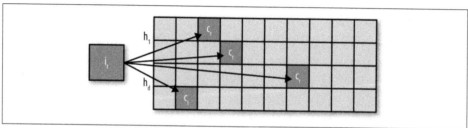

Figure 5-4. The count-min sketch

Guarding against data leakage

Since bin counting relies on historical data to generate the necessary statistics, it requires waiting through a data collection period, incurring a slight delay in the learning pipeline. Also, when the data distribution changes, the counts need to be updated. The faster the data changes, the more frequently the counts need to be recomputed. This is particularly important for applications like targeted advertising, where user preferences and popular queries change very quickly, and lack of adaptation to the current distribution could mean huge losses for the advertising platform.

One might ask, why not use the same dataset to compute the relevant statistics and train the model? The idea seems innocent enough. The big problem here is that the statistics involve the target variable, which is what the model tries to predict. Using the output to compute the input features leads to a pernicious problem known as *leakage*. In short, leakage means that information is revealed to the model that gives it an unrealistic advantage to make better predictions. This could happen when test data is leaked into the training set, or when data from the future is leaked to the past. Any time that a model is given information that it shouldn't have access to when it is making predictions in real time in production, there is leakage. Kaggle's wiki (*https:// www.kaggle.com/wiki/Leakage*) gives more examples of leakage and why it is bad for machine learning applications.

If the bin-counting procedure used the current data point's label to compute part of the input statistic, that would constitute direct leakage. One way to prevent that is by instituting strict separation between count collection (for computing bin-count statistics) and training, as illustrated in Figure 5-5—i.e., use an earlier batch of data points for counting, use the current data points for training (mapping categorical variables to historical statistics we just collected), and use future data points for testing. This fixes the problem of leakage, but introduces the aforementioned delay (the input statistics and therefore the model will trail behind current data).

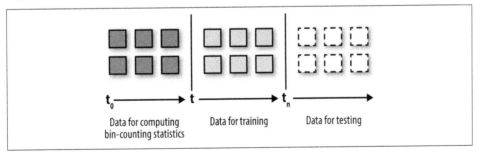

Figure 5-5. Using time windows can prevent data leakage during bin counting

It turns out that there is another solution, based on differential privacy. A statistic is *approximately leakage-proof* if its distribution stays roughly the same with or without any one data point. In practice, adding a small random noise with distribution Laplace(0,1) is sufficient to cover up any potential leakage from a single data point. This idea can be combined with leaving-one-out counting to formulate statistics on current data (Zhang, 2015).

Counts without bounds

If the statistics are updated continuously given more and more historical data, the raw counts will grow without bounds. This could be a problem for the model. A trained model "knows" the input data up to the observed scale. A trained decision tree might say, "When x is greater than 3, predict 1." A trained linear model might say, "Multiply x by 0.7 and see if the result is greater than the global average." These might be the correct decisions when x lies between 0 and 5. But what happens beyond that? No one knows.

When the input counts increase, the model will need to be retrained to adapt to the current scale. If the counts accumulate rather slowly, then the effective scale won't change too fast, and the model will not need to be retrained too frequently. But when counts increment very quickly, frequent retraining will be a nuisance.

For this reason, it is often better to use normalized counts that are guaranteed to be bounded in a known interval. For instance, the estimated click-through probability is bounded between [0, 1]. Another method is to take the log transform, which imposes a strict bound, but the rate of increase will be very slow when the count is very large.

Neither method will guard against shifting input distributions (e.g., last year's Barbie dolls are now out of style and people will no longer click on those ads). The model will need to be retrained to accommodate these more fundamental changes in input data distribution, or the whole pipeline will need to move to an online learning setting where the model is continuously adapting to the input.

Summary

Each of the approaches detailed in this chapter has its pros and cons. Here is a rundown of the trade-offs.

Plain one-hot encoding	
Space requirement	$O(n)$ using the sparse vector format, where n is the number of data points
Computation requirement	$O(nk)$ under a linear model, where k is the number of categories
Pros	• Easiest to implement • Potentially most accurate • Feasible for online learning

Plain one-hot encoding

Cons	• Computationally inefficient
	• Does not adapt to growing categories
	• Not feasible for anything other than linear models
	• Requires large-scale distributed optimization with truly large datasets

Feature hashing

Space requirement	$O(n)$ using the sparse matrix format, where n is the number of data points
Computation requirement	$O(nm)$ under a linear or kernel model, where m is the number of hash bins
Pros	• Easy to implement
	• Makes model training cheaper
	• Easily adaptable to new categories
	• Easily handles rare categories
	• Feasible for online learning
Cons	• Only suitable for linear or kernelized models
	• Hashed features not interpretable
	• Mixed reports of accuracy

Bin-counting

Space requirement	$O(n+k)$ for small, dense representation of each data point, plus the count statistics that must be kept for each category
Computation requirement	$O(n)$ for linear models; also usable for nonlinear models such as trees
Pros	• Smallest computational burden at training time
	• Enables tree-based models
	• Relatively easy to adapt to new categories
	• Handles rare categories with back-off or count-min sketch
	• Interpretable
Cons	• Requires historical data
	• Delayed updates required, not completely suitable for online learning
	• Higher potential for leakage

As we can see, none of the methods are perfect. Which one to use depends on the desired model. Linear models are cheaper to train and therefore can handle noncompressed representations such as one-hot encoding. Tree-based models, on the other hand, need to do repeated searches over all features for the right split, and are thus limited to small representations such as bin counting. Feature hashing sits in between those two extremes, but with mixed reports on the resulting accuracy.

Bibliography

Agarwal, Alekh, Oliveier Chapelle, Miroslav Dudík, and John Langford. "A Reliable Effective Terascale Linear Learning System." *Journal of Machine Learning Research* 15 (2015): 1111–1133.

Bilenko, Misha. "Big Learning Made Easy—with Counts!" Cortana Intelligence and Machine Learning Blog, February 17, 2015. *https://blogs.technet.microsoft.com/machinelearning/2015/02/17/big-learning-made-easy-with-counts/.*

Chen, Ye, Dmitry Pavlov, and John F. Canny. "Large-Scale Behavioral Targeting." *Proceedings of the 15th ACM SIGKDD International Conference on Knowledge Discovery and Data Mining* (2009): 209–218.

Cormode, Graham, and S. Muthukrishnan. "An Improved Data Stream Summary: The Count-Min Sketch and Its Applications." *Algorithms* 55 (2005): 29–38.

Graepel, Thore, Joaquin Quiñonero Candela, Thomas Borchert, and Ralf Herbrich. "Web-Scale Bayesian Click-Through Rate Prediction for Sponsored Search Advertising in Microsoft's Bing Search Engine." *Proceedings of the 27th International Conference on Machine Learning* (2010): 13–20.

He, Xinran, Junfeng Pan, Ou Jin, Tianbing Xu, Bo Liu, Tao Xu, Yanxin Shi, Antoine Atallah, Ralf Herbrich, Stuart Bowers, and Joaquin Quiñonero Candela. "Practical Lessons from Predicting Clicks on Ads at Facebook." *Proceedings of the 8th International Workshop on Data Mining for Online Advertising* (2014): 1–9.

Lee, Wenke, Salvatore J. Stolfo, and Kui W. Mok. 1998. "Mining Audit Data to Build Intrusion Detection Models." *Proceedings of the 4th ACM SIGKDD International Conference on Knowledge Discovery and Data Mining* (1998): 66–72.

Li, Wei, Xuerui Wang, Ruofei Zhang, Ying Cui, Jianchang Mao, and Rong Jin. "Exploitation and Exploration in a Performance Based Contextual Advertising System." *Proceedings of the 16th ACM SIGKDD International Conference on Knowledge Discovery and Data Mining* (2010): 27–36.

McMahan, H. Brendan, Gary Holt, D. Sculley, Michael Young, Dietmar Ebner, Julian Grady, Lan Nie, Todd Phillips, Eugene Davydov, Daniel Golovin, Sharat Chikkerur, Dan Liu, Martin Wattenberg, Arnar Mar Hrafnkelsson, Tom Boulos, and Jeremy Kubica. "Ad Click Prediction: A View from the Trenches." *Proceedings of the 19th ACM SIGKDD International Conference on Knowledge Discovery and Data Mining* (2013): 1222–1230.

Weinberger, Kilian, Anirban Dasgupta, Josh Attenberg, John Langford, and Alex Smola. 2009. "Feature Hashing for Large Scale Multitask Learning." *Proceedings of the 26th International Conference on Machine Learning* (2009): 1113–1120.

Yeh, Tse-Yu, and Yale N. Patt. "Two-Level Adaptive Training Branch Prediction." *Proceedings of the 24th Annual International Symposium on Microarchitecture* (1991): 51–61.

Zhang, Owen. 2015. "Tips for data science competitions." SlideShare presentation. Retrieved from *http://bit.ly/2DjuhBD*.

## CHAPTER 6

Dimensionality Reduction: Squashing the Data Pancake with PCA

With automatic data collection and feature generation techniques, one can quickly obtain a large number of features. But not all of them are useful. In Chapters 3 and 4, we discussed frequency-based filtering and feature scaling as ways of pruning away uninformative features. Now we will take a close look at the topic of feature dimensionality reduction using *principal component analysis* (PCA).

This chapter marks an entry into model-based feature engineering techniques. Prior to this point, most of the techniques can be defined without referencing the data. For instance, frequency-based filtering might say, "Get rid of all counts that are smaller than *n*," a procedure that can be carried out without further input from the data itself.

Model-based techniques, on the other hand, require information from the data. For example, PCA is defined around the principal axes of the data. In previous chapters, there was always a clear-cut line between data, features, and models. From this point forward, the difference gets increasingly blurry. This is exactly where the excitement lies in current research on feature learning.

Intuition

Dimensionality reduction is about getting rid of "uninformative information" while retaining the crucial bits. There are many ways to define "uninformative." PCA focuses on the notion of linear dependency. In "The Anatomy of a Matrix" on page 182, we describe the column space of a data matrix as the span of all feature vectors. If the column space is small compared to the total number of features, then most of the features are linear combinations of a few key features. Linearly dependent features are a waste of space and computation power because the information could have been encoded in much fewer features. To avoid this situation, principal component analysis tries to reduce such "fluff" by squashing the data into a much lower-dimensional linear subspace.

Picture the set of data points in feature space. Each data point is a dot, and the whole set of data points forms a blob. In Figure 6-1(a), the data points spread out evenly across both feature dimensions, and the blob fills the space. In this example, the column space has full rank. However, if some of those features are linear combinations of others, then the blob won't look so plump; it will look more like Figure 6-1(b), a flat blob where feature 1 is a duplicate (or a scalar multiple) of feature 2. In this case, we say that the *intrinsic dimensionality* of the blob is 1, even though it lies in a two-dimensional feature space.

In practice, things are rarely exactly equal to one another. It is more likely that we see features that are very close to being equal, but not quite. In such a case, the data blob might look something like Figure 6-1(c). It's an emaciated blob. If we wanted to reduce the number of features to pass to the model, then we could replace feature 1 and feature 2 with a new feature, maybe called feature 1.5, which lies on the diagonal line between the original two features. The original dataset could then be adequately represented by one number—the position along the direction of feature 1.5—instead of two numbers, *f1* and *f2*.

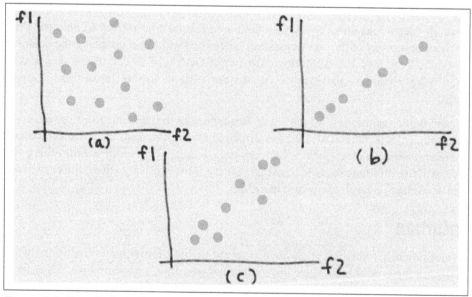

Figure 6-1. Data blobs in feature space: (a) full-rank data blob, (b) low-dimensional data blob, and (c) approximately low-dimensional data blob

The key idea here is to *replace redundant features with a few new features that adequately summarize information contained in the original feature space*. It's easy to tell what the new feature should be when there are only two features. It's much harder when the original feature space has hundreds or thousands of dimensions. We need a way to mathematically describe the new features we are looking for. Then we can use optimization techniques to find them.

One way to mathematically define "adequately summarize information" is to say that the new data blob should retain as much of the original volume as possible. We are squashing the data blob into a flat pancake, but we want the pancake to be as big as possible in the right directions. This means we need a way to measure volume.

Volume has to do with distance. But the notion of distance in a blob of data points is somewhat fuzzy. One could measure the maximum distance between any two pairs of points, but that turns out to be a very difficult function to mathematically optimize. An alternative is to measure the average distance between pairs of points, or equivalently, the average distance between each point and its mean, which is the variance. This turns out to be much easier to optimize. (Life is hard. Statisticians have learned to take convenient shortcuts.) Mathematically, this translates into maximizing the variance of the data points in the new feature space.

Tips for Navigating Linear Algebra Formulas

To stay oriented in the world of linear algebra, keep track of which quantities are scalars, which are vectors, and which way the vectors are oriented—vertically or horizontally. Know the dimensions of your matrices, because they often tell you whether the vectors of interest are in the rows or columns. Draw the matrices and vectors as rectangles on a page and make sure the shapes match. Just as one can get far in algebra by noting the units of measurement (distance is in miles, speed is in miles per hour), in linear algebra all one needs are the dimensions.

Derivation

As before, let X denote the $n \times d$ data matrix, where n is the number of data points and d the number of features. Let $\mathbf{x}$ be a column vector containing a single data point. (So $\mathbf{x}$ is the transpose of one of the rows in X.) Let $\mathbf{v}$ denote one of the new feature vectors, or principal components, that we are trying to find.

Linear Projection

Let's break down the derivation of PCA step by step. Figure 6-2 illustrates the whole process.

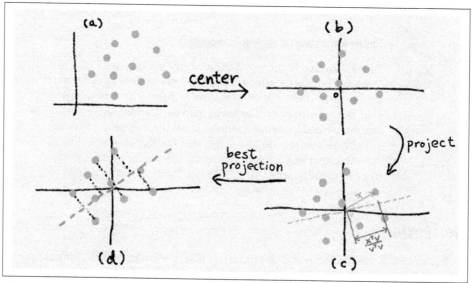

Figure 6-2. Illustration of PCA: (a) original data in feature space; (b) centered data; (c) projecting a data vector x onto another vector v; (d) direction of maximum variance of the projected coordinates (equal to the principal eigenvector of $X^T X$)

PCA uses linear projection to transform data into the new feature space. Figure 6-2(c) illustrates what a linear projection looks like. When we project **x** onto **v**, the length of the projection is proportional to the inner product between the two, normalized by the norm of **v** (its inner product with itself). Later on, we will constrain **v** to have unit norm. So, the only relevant part is the numerator—let's call it **v** (see Equation 6-1).

Equation 6-1. Projection coordinate

$$z = \mathbf{x}^T\mathbf{v}$$

Note that z is a scalar, whereas **x** and **v** are column vectors. Since there are a bunch of data points, we can formulate the vector **z** of all of their projection coordinates on the new feature **v** (Equation 6-2). Here, **X** is the familiar data matrix where each row is a data point. The resulting **z** is a column vector.

Equation 6-2. Vector of projection coordinates

$$\mathbf{z} = \mathbf{Xv}$$

Variance and Empirical Variance

The next step is to compute the variance of the projections. Variance is defined as the expectation of the squared distance to the mean (Equation 6-3).

Equation 6-3. Variance of a random variable Z

$$\mathrm{Var}(Z) = \mathrm{E}[Z - \mathrm{E}(Z)]^2$$

There is one tiny problem: our formulation of the problem says nothing about the mean, $E(Z)$; it is a free variable. One solution is to remove it from the equation by subtracting the mean from every data point. The resulting dataset has mean zero, which means that the variance is simply the expectation of Z^2. Geometrically, subtracting the mean has the effect of centering the data. (See Figure 6-2(a-b).)

A closely related quantity is the covariance between two random variables Z^1 and Z^2 (Equation 6-4). Think of this as the extension of the idea of variance (of a single random variable) to two random variables.

Equation 6-4. Covariance between two random variables Z^1 and Z^2

$$\mathrm{Cov}(Z^1, Z^2) = \mathrm{E}[(Z^1 - \mathrm{E}(Z^1)(Z^2 - \mathrm{E}(Z^2)]$$

When the random variables have mean zero, their covariance coincides with their *linear correlation*, $E[Z_1 Z_2]$. We will discuss this concept more later on.

Statistical quantities like variance and expectation are defined on a data distribution. In practice, we don't have the true distribution, but only a bunch of observed data points, z_1, ..., z_n. This is called an *empirical distribution*, and it gives us an empirical estimate of the variance (Equation 6-5).

Equation 6-5. Empirical variance of Z based on observations z

$$\text{Var}_{\text{emp}}(Z) = \frac{1}{n-1} \sum_{i=1}^{n} z_i^2$$

Principal Components: First Formulation

Combined with the definition of z_i in Equation 6-1, we have the formulation for maximizing the variance of the projected data given in Equation 6-6. (We drop the denominator $n-1$ from the definition of empirical variance, because it is a global constant and does not affect where the maximizing value occurs.)

Equation 6-6. Objective function of principal components

$$\max_{\mathbf{w}} \sum_{i=1}^{n} (\mathbf{x}_i^T \mathbf{w})^2, \quad \text{where } \mathbf{w}^T \mathbf{w} = 1$$

The constraint here forces the inner product of $\mathbf{w}$ with itself to be 1, which is equivalent to saying that the vector must have unit length. This is because we only care about the direction and not the magnitude of $\mathbf{w}$. The magnitude of $\mathbf{w}$ is an unnecessary degree of freedom, so we get rid of it by setting it to an arbitrary value.

Principal Components: Matrix-Vector Formulation

Next comes the tricky step. The sum of squares term in Equation 6-6 is rather cumbersome. It'd be much cleaner in a matrix-vector format. Can we do it? The answer is yes. The key lies in the sum-of-squares identity: the sum of a bunch of squared terms is equal to the squared norm of a vector whose elements are those terms, which is equivalent to the vector's inner product with itself. With this identity in hand, we can rewrite Equation 6-6 in matrix-vector notation, as shown in Equation 6-7.

Equation 6-7. Objective function for principal components, matrix-vector formulation

$$\max_{\mathbf{w}} \mathbf{w}^T \mathbf{w}, \quad \text{where } \mathbf{w}^T \mathbf{w} = 1$$

This formulation of PCA presents the target more clearly: we look for an input direction that maximizes the norm of the output. Does this sound familiar? The answer lies in the *singular value decomposition* (SVD) of X. The optimal $\mathbf{w}$, as it turns out, is the principal left singular vector of X, which is also the principal eigenvector of X^TX. The projected data is called a principal component of the original data.

General Solution of the Principal Components

This process can be repeated. Once we find the first principal component, we can rerun Equation 6-7 with the added constraint that the new vector be orthogonal to the previously found vectors (see Equation 6-8).

Equation 6-8. Objective function for k+1st principal components

$\max_w \mathbf{w}^T\mathbf{w}$, where $\mathbf{w}^T\mathbf{w} = 1$ and $\mathbf{w}^T\mathbf{w}_1 = ... = \mathbf{w}^T\mathbf{w}_k = 0$

The solution is the $k+1$st left singular vectors of X, ordered by descending singular values. Thus, the first k principal components correspond to the first k left singular vectors of X.

Transforming Features

Once the principal components are found, we can transform the features using linear projection. Let $X = U\Sigma V^T$ be the SVD of X, and V_k the matrix whose columns contain the first k left singular vectors. X has dimensions $n \times d$, where d is the number of original features, and V_k has dimensions $d \times k$. Instead of a single projection vector as in Equation 6-2, we can simultaneously project onto multiple vectors in a projection matrix (Equation 6-9).

Equation 6-9. PCA projection matrix

$W = V_k$

The matrix of projected coordinates is easy to compute, and can be further simplified using the fact that the singular vectors are orthogonal to each other (see Equation 6-10).

Equation 6-10. Simple PCA transform

$Z = XW = XV_k = U\Sigma V^TV_k = U_k\Sigma_k$

The projected values are simply the first k right singular vectors scaled by the first k singular values. Thus, the entire PCA solution, components and projections alike, can be conveniently obtained through the SVD of X.

Implementing PCA

Many derivations of PCA involve first centering the data, then taking the eigen decomposition of the covariance matrix. But the easiest way to implement PCA is by taking the singular value decomposition of the centered data matrix.

PCA Implementation Steps

1. Center the data matrix:

$$C = X - \mathbf{1}\mu^T$$

where $\mathbf{1}$ is a column vector containing all 1s, and μ is a column vector containing the average of the rows of X.

2. Compute the SVD:

$$C = U\Sigma V^T$$

3. Find the principal components. The first k principal components are the first k columns of V; i.e., the right singular vectors corresponding to the k largest singular values.

4. Transform the data. The transformed data is simply the first k columns of U. (If whitening is desired, then scale the vectors by the inverse singular values. This requires that the selected singular values are nonzero. See "Whitening and ZCA" on page 108.)

PCA in Action

Let's get a better sense for how PCA works by applying it to some image data. The MNIST dataset (*http://yann.lecun.com/exdb/mnist/*) contains images of handwritten digits from 0 to 9. The original images are 28 × 28 pixels. A lower-resolution subset of the images is distributed with scikit-learn (*http://bit.ly/2G3A3dA*), where each image is downsampled into 8 × 8 pixels. The original data in scikit-learn has 64 dimensions. In Example 6-1, we apply PCA and visualize the dataset using the first three principal components.

Example 6-1. Principal component analysis of the scikit-learn digits dataset (a subset of the MNIST dataset)

```
>>> from sklearn import datasets
>>> from sklearn.decomposition import PCA
```

```
# Load the data
>>> digits_data = datasets.load_digits()
>>> n = len(digits_data.images)

# Each image is represented as an 8-by-8 array.
# Flatten this array as input to PCA.
>>> image_data = digits_data.images.reshape((n, -1))
>>> image_data.shape
(1797, 64)

# Groundtruth label of the number appearing in each image
>>> labels = digits_data.target
>>> labels
array([0, 1, 2, ..., 8, 9, 8])

# Fit a PCA transformer to the dataset.
# The number of components is automatically chosen to account for
# at least 80% of the total variance.
>>> pca_transformer = PCA(n_components=0.8)
>>> pca_images = pca_transformer.fit_transform(image_data)
>>> pca_transformer.explained_variance_ratio_
array([ 0.14890594,  0.13618771,  0.11794594,  0.08409979,  0.05782415,
        0.0491691 ,  0.04315987,  0.03661373,  0.03353248,  0.03078806,
        0.02372341,  0.02272697,  0.01821863])
>>> pca_transformer.explained_variance_ratio_[:3].sum()
0.40303958587675121

# Visualize the results
>>> import matplotlib.pyplot as plt
>>> from mpl_toolkits.mplot3d import Axes3D
>>> %matplotlib notebook
>>> fig = plt.figure()
>>> ax = fig.add_subplot(111, projection='3d')
>>> for i in range(100):
...     ax.scatter(pca_images[i,0], pca_images[i,1], pca_images[i,2],
...                marker=r'${}$'.format(labels[i]), s=64)

>>> ax.set_xlabel('Principal component 1')
>>> ax.set_ylabel('Principal component 2')
>>> ax.set_zlabel('Principal component 3')
```

The first 100 projected images are shown in a 3D plot in Figure 6-3. The markers correspond to the labels. The first three principal components account for roughly 40% of the total variance in the dataset. This is by no means perfect, but it allows for a handy low-dimensional visualization. We see that PCA groups similar numbers close to each other. The numbers 0 and 6 lie in the same region, as do 1 and 7, and 3 and 9. The space is roughly divided between 0, 4, and 6 on one side, and the rest of the numbers on the other.

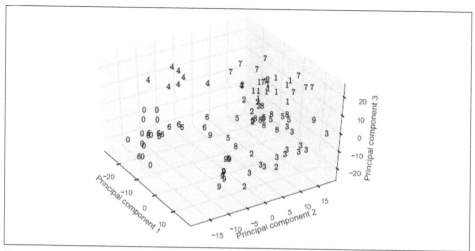

Figure 6-3. PCA projections of subset of MNIST data—markers correspond to image labels

Since there is a fair amount of overlap between numbers, it would be difficult to tell them apart using a linear classifier in the projected space. Hence, if the task is to classify the handwritten digits and the chosen model is a linear classifier, then the first three principal components are not sufficient as features. Nevertheless, it is interesting to see how much of a 64-dimensional dataset can be captured in just 3 dimensions.

Whitening and ZCA

Due to the orthogonality constraint in the objective function, PCA transformation produces a nice side effect: the transformed features are no longer correlated. In other words, the inner products between pairs of feature vectors are zero. It's easy to prove this using the orthogonality property of the singular vectors:

$$\mathbf{Z}^T\mathbf{Z} = \Sigma_k \mathbf{U}_k^T \mathbf{U}_k \Sigma_k = \Sigma_k^2$$

The result is a diagonal matrix containing squares of the singular values representing the correlation of each feature vector with itself, also known as its ℓ^2 norm.

Sometimes, it is useful to also normalize the scale of the features to 1. In signal processing terms, this is known as *whitening*. It results in a set of features that have unit correlation with themselves and zero correlation with each other. Mathematically, whitening can done by multiplying the PCA transformation with the inverse singular values (see Equation 6-11).

Equation 6-11. PCA + whitening

$$W_{white} = V_k \Sigma_k^{-1}$$

$$Z_{white} = XV_k \Sigma_k^{-1} = U\Sigma V^T V_k \Sigma_k^{-1} = U_k$$

Whitening is independent from dimensionality reduction; one can perform one without the other. For example, *zero-phase component analysis* (ZCA) (Bell and Sejnowski, 1996) is a whitening transformation that is closely related to PCA, but that does not reduce the number of features. ZCA whitening uses the full set of principal components V without reduction, and includes an extra multiplication back onto V^T (Equation 6-12).

Equation 6-12. ZCA whitening

$$W_{ZCA} = V\Sigma^{-1}V^T$$

$$Z_{zca} = XV\Sigma^{-1}V^T = U\Sigma V^T V\Sigma^{-1} = U$$

Simple PCA projection (Equation 6-10) produces coordinates in the new feature space, where the principal components serve as the basis. These coordinates represent only the length of the projected vector, not the direction. Multiplication with the principal components gives us the length and the orientation. Another valid interpretation is that the extra multiplication rotates the coordinates back into the original feature space. (V is an orthogonal matrix, and orthogonal matrices rotate their input without stretching or compression.) So, ZCA produces whitened data that is as close (in Euclidean distance) to the original data as possible.

Considerations and Limitations of PCA

When using PCA for dimensionality reduction, one must address the question of how many principal components (k) to use. Like all hyperparameters, this number can be tuned based on the quality of the resulting model. But there are also heuristics that do not involve expensive computational methods.

One possibility is to pick k to account for a desired proportion of total variance. (This option is available in the scikit-learn package PCA.) The variance of the projection onto the kth component is:

$$\| Xv_k \|^2 = \| u_k \sigma_k \|^2 = \sigma_k^2$$

which is the square of the kth-largest singular value of X. The ordered list of singular values of a matrix is called its *spectrum*. Thus, to determine how many components to use, one can perform a simple spectral analysis of the data matrix and pick the threshold that retains enough variance.

Selecting k Based on Accounted Variance

To retain enough components to cover 80% of the total variance in the data, pick k such that

$$\frac{\sum_{i=1}^{k} \sigma_i^2}{\sum_{i=1}^{d} \sigma_i^2} \geq 0.8.$$

Another method for picking k involves the intrinsic dimensionality of a dataset. This is a hazier concept, but can also be determined from the spectrum. Basically, if the spectrum contains a few large singular values and a number of tiny ones, then one can probably just harvest the largest singular values and discard the rest. Sometimes the rest of the spectrum is not tiny, but there's a large gap between the head and the tail values. That would also be a reasonable cutoff. This method is requires visual inspection of the spectrum and hence cannot be performed as part of an automated pipeline.

One key criticism of PCA is that the transformation is fairly complex, and the results are therefore hard to interpret. The principal components and the projected vectors are real-valued and could be positive or negative. The principal components are essentially linear combinations of the (centered) rows, and the projection values are linear combinations of the columns. In a stock returns application, for instance, each factor is a linear combination of time slices of stock returns. What does that mean? It is hard to express a human-understandable reason for the learned factors. Therefore, it is hard for analysts to trust the results. If you can't explain why you should be putting billions of other people's money into particular stocks, you probably won't choose to use that model.

PCA is computationally expensive. It relies on SVD, which is an expensive procedure. To compute the full SVD of a matrix takes $O(nd^2 + d^3)$ operations (Golub and Van Loan, 2012), assuming $n \geq d$—i.e., there are more data points than features. Even if we only want k principal components, computing the truncated SVD (the k largest singular values and vectors) still takes $O((n+d)^2 k) = O(n^2k)$ operations. This is prohibitive when there are a large number of data points or features.

It is difficult to perform PCA in a streaming fashion, in batch updates, or from a sample of the full data. Streaming computation of the SVD, updating the SVD, and computing the SVD from a subsample are all difficult research problems. Algorithms exist, but at the cost of reduced accuracy. One implication is that one should expect lower representational accuracy when projecting test data onto principal components found in the training set. As the distribution of the data changes, one would have to recompute the principal components in the current dataset.

Lastly, it is best not to apply PCA to raw counts (word counts, music play counts, movie viewing counts, etc.). The reason for this is that such counts often contain large outliers. (The probability is pretty high that there is a fan out there who watched *The Lord of the Rings* 314,582 times, which dwarfs the rest of the counts.) As we know, PCA looks for linear correlations within the features. Correlation and variance statistics are very sensitive to large outliers; a single large number could change the statistics a lot. So, it is a good idea to first trim the data of large values ("Frequency-Based Filtering" on page 48), or apply a scaling transform like tf-idf (Chapter 4) or the log transform ("Log Transformation" on page 15).

Use Cases

PCA reduces feature space dimensionality by looking for linear correlation patterns between features. Since it involves the SVD, PCA is expensive to compute for more than a few thousand features. But for small numbers of real-valued features, it is very much worth trying.

PCA transformation discards information from the data. Thus, the downstream model may be cheaper to train, but less accurate. On the MNIST dataset, some have observed that using reduced-dimensionality data from PCA results in less accurate classification models. In these cases, there is both an upside and a downside to using PCA.

One of the coolest applications of PCA is in anomaly detection of time series. Lakhina et al. (2004) used PCA to detect and diagnose anomalies in internet traffic. They focused on volume anomalies, i.e., when there is a surge or a dip in the amount of traffic going from one network region to another. These sudden changes may be indicative of a misconfigured network or coordinated denial-of-service attacks. Either way, knowing when and where such changes occur is valuable to internet operators.

Since there is so much total traffic over the internet, isolated surges in small regions are hard to detect. A relatively small set of backbone links handle much of the traffic. Their key insight is that volume anomalies affect multiple links at the same time (because network packets need to hop through multiple nodes to reach their destination). Treat each of the links as a feature, and the amount of traffic at each time step as the measurement. A data point is a time slice of traffic measurements across all links on the network. The principal components of this matrix indicate the overall traffic trends on the network. The rest of the components represent the residual signal, which contains the anomalies.

PCA is also often used in financial modeling. In those use cases, it works as a type of *factor analysis*, a term that describes a family of statistical methods that aim to describe observed variability in data using a small number of unobserved factors. In factor analysis applications, the goal is to find the explanatory components, not the transformed data.

Financial quantities like stock returns are often correlated with each other. Stocks may move up and down at the same time (positive correlation), or move in opposite directions (negative correlation). In order to balance volatility and reduce risk, an investment portfolio needs a diverse set of stocks that are not correlated with each other. (Don't put all your eggs in one basket if that basket is going to sink.) Finding strong correlation patterns is helpful for deciding on an investment strategy.

Stock correlation patterns can be industry-wide. For example, tech stocks may go up and down together, while airline stocks tend to go down when oil prices are high. But industry may not be the best way to explain the outcome. Analysts also look for unexpected correlations in observed statistics. In particular, the *statistical factor model* (Connor, 1995) runs PCA on the matrix of time series of individual stock returns to find commonly covarying stocks. In this use case, the end goal is the principal components themselves, not the transformed data.

ZCA is useful as a preprocessing step when learning from images. In natural images, adjacent pixels often have similar colors. ZCA whitening can remove this correlation, which allows subsequent modeling efforts to focus on more interesting image structures. Krizhevsky's (2009) thesis on "Learning Multiple Layers of Features from Images" (*http://bit.ly/2ts42tc*) contains nice examples that illustrate the effect of ZCA whitening on natural images.

Many deep learning models use PCA or ZCA as a preprocessing step, though it is not always necessary. In "Factored 3-Way Restricted Boltzmann Machines for Modeling Natural Images" (*http://bit.ly/2D7hKkK*), Ranzato et al. (2010) remark, "Whitening is not necessary but speeds up the convergence of the algorithm." In "An Analysis of Single-Layer Networks in Unsupervised Feature Learning" (*http://stanford.io/2oVhBvu*), Coates et al. (2011) find that ZCA whitening is helpful for some models, but not all. (Note the models in this paper are unsupervised feature learning models, so ZCA is used as a feature engineering method for other feature engineering methods. Stacking and chaining of methods is common in machine learning pipelines.)

Summary

This concludes the discussion of PCA. The two main things to remember about PCA are its mechanism (linear projection) and objective (to maximize the variance of projected data). The solution involves the eigen decomposition of the covariance matrix, which is closely related to the SVD of the data matrix. One can also remember PCA with the mental picture of squashing the data into a pancake that is as fluffy as possible.

PCA is an example of model-driven feature engineering. (One should immediately suspect that a model is lurking in the background whenever an objective function enters the scene.) The modeling assumption here is that variance adequately represents the information contained in the data. Equivalently, the model looks for linear correlations between features. This is used in several applications to reduce the correlation or find common factors in the input.

PCA is a well-known dimensionality reduction method. But it has its limitations, such as high computational cost and uninterpretable outcome. It is useful as a preprocessing step, especially when there are linear correlations between features.

When seen as a method for eliminating linear correlation, PCA is related to the concept of whitening. Its cousin, ZCA, whitens the data in an interpretable way, but does not reduce dimensionality.

Bibliography

Bell, Anthony J. and Terrence J. Sejnowski. "Edges Are the 'Independent Components' of Natural Scenes." *Advances in Neural Information Processing Systems* 9 (1996): 831–837.

Coates, Adam, Andrew Y. Ng, and Honglak Lee. "An Analysis of Single-Layer Networks in Unsupervised Feature Learning." *Proceedings of the 14th International conference on Artificial Intelligence and Statistics* (2011): 215–223.

Connor, Gregory. "The Three Types of Factor Models: A Comparison of Their Explanatory Power." *Financial Analysts Journal* 51:3 (1995) 42–46.

Golub, Gene H., and Charles F. Van Loan. *Matrix Computations.* 4th ed. Baltimore, MD: Johns Hopkins University Press, 2012.

Krizhevsky, Alex. "Learning Multiple Layers of Features from Tiny Images." MSc thesis, University of Toronto, 2009.

Lakhina, Anukool, Mark Crovella, and Christophe Diot. "Diagnosing Network-wide Traffic Anomalies." *Proceedings of the 2004 Conference on Applications, Technologies, Architectures, and Protocols for Computer Communications* (2004): 219–230.

Ranzato, Marc'Aurelio, Alex Krizhevsky, and Geoffrey E. Hinton. "Factored 3-Way Restricted Boltzmann Machines for Modeling Natural Images." *Proceedings of the 13th International Conference on Artificial Intelligence and Statistics* (2010): 621–628.

## CHAPTER 7

Nonlinear Featurization via K-Means Model Stacking

PCA is very useful when the data lies in a linear subspace like a flat pancake. But what if the data forms a more complicated shape?[1] A flat plane (linear subspace) can be generalized to a *manifold* (nonlinear subspace), which can be thought of as a surface that gets stretched and rolled in various ways.[2]

If a linear subspace is a flat sheet of paper, then a rolled up sheet of paper is a simple example of a nonlinear manifold. Informally, this is called a *Swiss roll* (see Figure 7-1). Once rolled, a 2D plane occupies 3D space. Yet it is essentially still a 2D object. In other words, it has low intrinsic dimensionality, a concept we've already touched upon in "Intuition" on page 99. If we could somehow unroll the Swiss roll, we'd recover the 2D plane. This is the goal of *nonlinear dimensionality reduction*, which assumes that the manifold is simpler than the full dimension it occupies and attempts to unfold it.

---

1 This chapter is inspired by a conversation with Ted Dunning (*http://www.oreilly.com/pub/au/5873*), active Apache contributor and noted author. The stacking example came directly from Ted, and he provided many helpful comments in the course of writing. If one could have coauthors for individual chapters, Ted would be a coauthor for this one.

2 We use the words "surface" and "manifold" interchangeably in this chapter. The analogy works well for two-dimensional manifolds embedded in a three-dimensional space, but it breaks down beyond three dimensions. A high-dimensional manifold does not conform to our usual notion of a "surface." Some of the more out-landish manifolds have holes, and some loop back onto themselves in a way that would never happen in the real physical world (e.g., M.C. Escher's endless waterfall). Most data models assume nice manifolds, not the crazy ones.

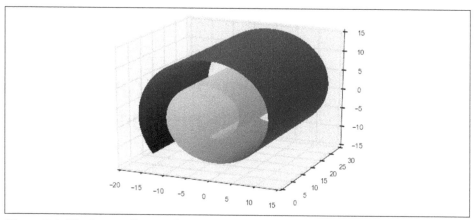

Figure 7-1. The Swiss roll, a nonlinear manifold

The key observation is that even when a big manifold looks complicated, the local neighborhood around each point can often be well approximated with a patch of flat surface. In other words, the patches to encode global structure using local structure.[3] Nonlinear dimensionality reduction is also called *nonlinear embedding* or *manifold learning*. Nonlinear embeddings are useful for aggressively compressing high-dimensional data into low-dimensional data. They are often used for visualization in two or three dimensions.

The goal of feature engineering, however, isn't so much to make the feature dimensions as low as possible, but to arrive at the *right* features for the task. In this chapter, the right features are those that represent the spatial characteristics of the data.

Clustering algorithms are usually not presented as techniques for local structure learning. But they in fact enable just that. Points that are close to each other (where "closeness" can be defined by a chosen metric) belong to the same cluster. Given a clustering, a data point can be represented by its cluster membership vector. If the number of clusters is smaller than the original number of features, then the new representation will have fewer dimensions than the original; the original data is compressed into a lower dimension. We will unpack this idea in this chapter.

Compared to nonlinear embedding techniques, clustering may produce more features. But if the end goal is feature engineering instead of visualization, this is not a problem.

---

3 This is a tried-and-true idea in mathematics. For instance, the derivative of a function measures the speed of change at each point. Globally, the function may do all sorts of weird things. But locally, it can be approximated by a linear function of the derivative. If we know the derivative at each point, then calculus allows us to more or less recover the entire original function.

We will illustrate the idea of local structure learning with a common clustering algorithm called k-means. It is simple to understand and implement. Instead of nonlinear manifold reduction, it is more apt to say that k-means performs *nonlinear manifold feature extraction*. Used correctly, it can be a powerful tool in our feature engineering repertoire.

k-Means Clustering

k-means is a clustering algorithm. Clustering algorithms group data depending on how they are laid out in space. They are *unsupervised* in that they do not require any sort of label—it's the algorithm's job to infer cluster labels based solely on the geometry of the data itself.

A clustering algorithm depends on a *metric*—a measurement of closeness between data points. The most popular metric is the Euclidean distance or Euclidean metric. It comes from Euclidean geometry and measures the straight-line distance between two points. It should feel very normal to us because this is the distance we see in everyday physical reality.

The Euclidean distance between two vectors x and y is the ℓ^2 norm of $x - y$. (See "ℓ^2 Normalization" on page 32 for more on the ℓ^2 norm.) In math speak, it is usually written as $\|x - y\|_2$ or just $\|x - y\|$.

k-means establishes a hard clustering, meaning that each data point is assigned to one and only one cluster. The algorithm learns to position the cluster centers such that the total sum of the Euclidean distance between each data point and its cluster center is minimized. For those who like to read math instead of words, here is the objective function:

$$\min_{C_1, \ldots, C_k, \mu_1, \ldots, \mu_k} \sum_{i=1}^{k} \sum_{x \in C_i} \| x - \mu_i \|_2$$

Each cluster C_i contains a subset of data points. The center of cluster i is equal to the average of all the data points in the cluster:

$$\mu_i = \sum_{x \in C_i} x / n_i$$

where n_i denotes the number of data points in cluster i.

Figure 7-2 shows *k*-means at work on two different, randomly generated datasets. The data in (a) is generated from random Gaussian distributions with the same variance but different means. The data in (c) is generated uniformly at random. These toy problems are very simple to solve, and *k*-means does a good job. (The results could be sensitive to the number of clusters, which must be given to the algorithm.)

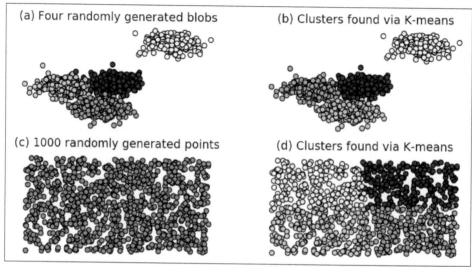

Figure 7-2. k-means examples demonstrating how the clustering algorithm partitions space

The code for this example is found in Example 7-1.

Example 7-1. Code to generate k-means examples

```
>>> import numpy as np
>>> from sklearn.cluster import KMeans
>>> from sklearn.datasets import make_blobs

>>> import matplotlib.pyplot as plt

>>> n_data = 1000
>>> seed = 1
>>> n_clusters = 4

# Generate random Gaussian blobs and run k-means
>>> blobs, blob_labels = make_blobs(n_samples=n_data, n_features=2,
...                                  centers=n_centers, random_state=seed)
>>> clusters_blob = KMeans(n_clusters=n_centers, random_state=seed).fit_predict(blobs)

# Generate data uniformly at random and run k-means
>>> uniform = np.random.rand(n_data, 2)
>>> clusters_uniform = KMeans(n_clusters=n_clusters,
```

```
...                      random_state=seed).fit_predict(uniform)

# Matplotlib incantations for visualizing results
>>> figure = plt.figure()
>>> plt.subplot(221)
>>> plt.scatter(blobs[:, 0], blobs[:, 1], c=blob_labels, cmap='gist_rainbow')
>>> plt.title("(a) Four randomly generated blobs", fontsize=14)
>>> plt.axis('off')

>>> plt.subplot(222)
>>> plt.scatter(blobs[:, 0], blobs[:, 1], c=clusters_blob, cmap='gist_rainbow')
>>> plt.title("(b) Clusters found via K-means", fontsize=14)
>>> plt.axis('off')

>>> plt.subplot(223)
>>> plt.scatter(uniform[:, 0], uniform[:, 1])
>>> plt.title("(c) 1000 randomly generated points", fontsize=14)
>>> plt.axis('off')

>>> plt.subplot(224)
>>> plt.scatter(uniform[:, 0], uniform[:, 1], c=clusters_uniform, cmap='gist_rainbow')
>>> plt.title("(d) Clusters found via K-means", fontsize=14)
>>> plt.axis('off')
```

Clustering as Surface Tiling

Common applications of clustering assume that there are natural clusters to be found; i.e., there are regions of dense data scattered in an otherwise empty space. In these situations, there is a notion of the correct number of clusters, and people have invented clustering indices that measure the quality of data groupings in order to select for k.

However, when data is spread out fairly uniformly like in Figure 7-2(c), there is no longer a correct number of clusters. In this case, the role of a clustering algorithm is *vector quantization*, i.e., partitioning the data into a finite number of chunks. The number of clusters can be selected based on acceptable approximation error when using quantized vectors instead of the original ones.

Visually, this usage of k-means can be thought of as covering the data surface with patches, like in Figure 7-3. This is indeed what we get if we run k-means on a Swiss roll dataset.

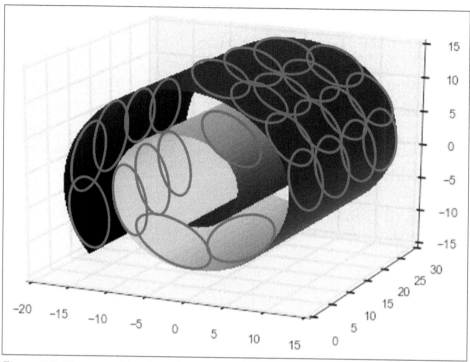

Figure 7-3. Conceptual local patches on the Swiss roll from a clustering algorithm

Example 7-2 uses scikit-learn to generate a noisy dataset on the Swiss roll, cluster it with *k*-means, and visualize the clustering results using Matplotlib. The data points are colored according to their cluster IDs.

Example 7-2. k-means on the Swiss roll

```
>>> from mpl_toolkits.mplot3d import Axes3D
>>> from sklearn import manifold, datasets

# Generate a noisy Swiss roll dataset
>>> X, color = datasets.samples_generator.make_swiss_roll(n_samples=1500)

# Approximate the data with 100 k-means clusters
>>> clusters_swiss_roll = KMeans(n_clusters=100, random_state=1).fit_predict(X)

# Plot the dataset with k-means cluster IDs as the color
>>> fig2 = plt.figure()
>>> ax = fig2.add_subplot(111, projection='3d')
>>> ax.scatter(X[:, 0], X[:, 1], X[:, 2], c=clusters_swiss_roll, cmap='Spectral')
```

In this example, we generated 1,500 points at random on the Swiss roll surface, and asked *k*-means to approximate it with 100 clusters. We pulled the number 100 out of a hat because it seems like a fairly large number to cover a fairly small space. The result (Figure 7-4) looks nice; the clusters are indeed very local and different sections of the manifold are mapped to different clusters. Great! Are we done?

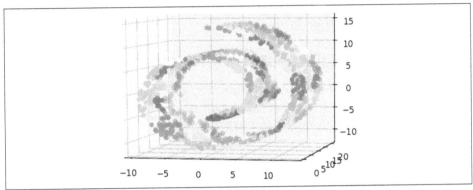

Figure 7-4. Approximating a Swiss roll dataset using k-means with 100 clusters

The problem is that if we pick a k that is too small, then the results won't be so nice from a manifold learning perspective. Figure 7-5 shows the output of k-means on the Swiss roll with 10 clusters. We can clearly see data from very different sections of the manifold being mapped to the same clusters (e.g., the yellow, purple, green, and magenta clusters—see, we told you the illustrations are best viewed in color!).

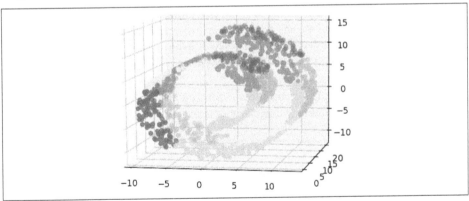

Figure 7-5. k-means on the Swiss roll with 10 clusters

If the data is distributed uniformly throughout the space, then picking the right k boils down to a sphere-packing problem. In d dimensions, one could fit roughly $1/r^d$ spheres of radius r. Each k-means cluster is a sphere, and the radius is the maximum error of representing points in that sphere with the centroid. So, if we are willing to tolerate a maximum approximation error of r per data point, then the number of clusters is $O(1/r^d)$, where d is the dimension of the original feature space of the data.

Uniform distribution is the worst-case scenario for k-means. If data density is not uniform, then we will be able to represent more data with fewer clusters. In general, it is difficult to tell how data is distributed in high-dimensional space. One can be conservative and pick a larger k, but it can't be too large, because k will become the number of features for the next modeling step.

k-Means Featurization for Classification

When using k-means as a featurization procedure, a data point can be represented by its cluster membership (a sparse one-hot encoding of the cluster membership categorical variable; see "One-Hot Encoding" on page 78), which we now illustrate.

If a target variable is also available, then we have the choice of giving that information as a hint to the clustering procedure. One way to incorporate target information is to simply include the target variable as an additional input feature to the k-means algorithm. Since the objective is to minimize the total Euclidean distance over all input dimensions, the clustering procedure will attempt to balance similarity in the target value as well as in the original feature space. The target values can be scaled to get more or less attention from the clustering algorithm. Larger differences in the target will produce clusters that pay more attention to the classification boundary.

k-Means Featurization

Clustering algorithms analyze the spatial distribution of data. Therefore, k-means featurization creates a compressed spatial index of the data which can be fed into the model in the next stage. This is an example of *model stacking*.

Example 7-3 shows a simple k-means featurizer. It is defined as a class object that can be fitted to training data and transform any new data.

Example 7-3. k-means featurizer

```
>>> import numpy as np
>>> from sklearn.cluster import KMeans

>>> class KMeansFeaturizer:
...     """Transforms numeric data into k-means cluster memberships.
...
...     This transformer runs k-means on the input data and converts each data point
...     into the ID of the closest cluster. If a target variable is present, it is
...     scaled and included as input to k-means in order to derive clusters that
...     obey the classification boundary as well as group similar points together.
...     """
...
...
...     def __init__(self, k=100, target_scale=5.0, random_state=None):
```

```
...            self.k = k
...            self.target_scale = target_scale
...            self.random_state = random_state
...
...        def fit(self, X, y=None):
...            """Runs k-means on the input data and finds centroids.
...            """
...            if y is None:
...                # No target variable, just do plain k-means
...                km_model = KMeans(n_clusters=self.k,
...                                  n_init=20,
...                                  random_state=self.random_state)
...                km_model.fit(X)
...
...                self.km_model_ = km_model
...                self.cluster_centers_ = km_model.cluster_centers_
...                return self
...
...            # There is target information. Apply appropriate scaling and include
...            # it in the input data to k-means.
...            data_with_target = np.hstack((X, y[:,np.newaxis]*self.target_scale))
...
...            # Build a pre-training k-means model on data and target
...            km_model_pretrain = KMeans(n_clusters=self.k,
...                                       n_init=20,
...                                       random_state=self.random_state)
...            km_model_pretrain.fit(data_with_target)
...
...            # Run k-means a second time to get the clusters in the original space
...            # without target info. Initialize using centroids found in pre-training.
...            # Go through a single iteration of cluster assignment and centroid
...            # recomputation.
...            km_model = KMeans(n_clusters=self.k,
...                              init=km_model_pretrain.cluster_centers_[:,:2],
...                              n_init=1,
...                              max_iter=1)
...            km_model.fit(X)
...
...            self.km_model = km_model
...            self.cluster_centers_ = km_model.cluster_centers_
...            return self
...
...        def transform(self, X, y=None):
...            """Outputs the closest cluster ID for each input data point.
...            """
...            clusters = self.km_model.predict(X)
...            return clusters[:,np.newaxis]
...
...        def fit_transform(self, X, y=None):
...            self.fit(X, y)
...            return self.transform(X, y)
```

To illustrate the difference between using and not using target information when clustering in Example 7-4, we apply the featurizer to a synthetic dataset generated using scikit-learn's make_moons function (*http://scikit-learn.org/stable/modules/gener ated/sklearn.datasets.make_moons.html*) and plot the Voronoi diagram of the cluster boundaries.

Example 7-4. k-means featurization with and without target hints

```
>>> from scipy.spatial import Voronoi, voronoi_plot_2d
>>> from sklearn.datasets import make_moons

>>> training_data, training_labels = make_moons(n_samples=2000, noise=0.2)
>>> kmf_hint = KMeansFeaturizer(k=100, target_scale=10).fit(training_data,
...                                                 training_labels)
>>> kmf_no_hint = KMeansFeaturizer(k=100, target_scale=0).fit(training_data,
...                                                 training_labels)

>>> def kmeans_voronoi_plot(X, y, cluster_centers, ax):
...     """Plots the Voronoi diagram of the k-means clusters overlaid with the data"""
...     ax.scatter(X[:, 0], X[:, 1], c=y, cmap='Set1', alpha=0.2)
...     vor = Voronoi(cluster_centers)
...     voronoi_plot_2d(vor, ax=ax, show_vertices=False, alpha=0.5)
```

Figure 7-6 shows a comparison of the results. The two moons of the dataset are colored according to their class labels. The bottom panel shows the clusters trained without target information. Notice that a number of clusters span the empty space between the two classes. The top panel shows that when the clustering algorithm is given target information, the cluster boundaries align much better along class boundaries.

Let's test the effectiveness of *k*-means features for classification. Example 7-5 applies logistic regression on the input data augmented with *k*-means cluster features. It compares the results against the support vector machine with radial basis function kernel (RBF SVM), *k*-nearest neighbors (*k*NN), random forest (RF), and gradient boosting tree (GBT) classifiers. RF and GBT are popular nonlinear classifiers with state-of-the-art performance. RBF SVM is a reasonable nonlinear classifier for Euclidean space. *k*NN classifies data according to the average of its *k* nearest neighbors.

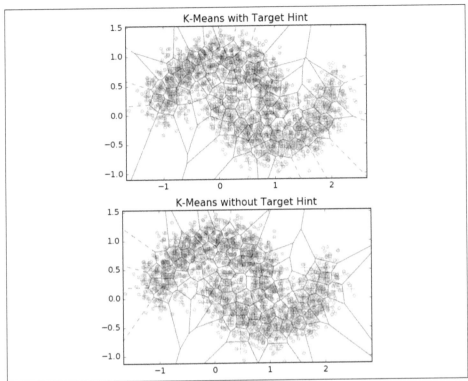

Figure 7-6. k-means clusters with (top panel) and without (bottom panel) using target class information

The default input data to the classifiers consists of the 2D coordinates of each data point. Logistic regression is also given the cluster membership features (labeled "LR with *k*-means" in Figure 7-7). As a baseline, we also try logistic regression on just the 2D coordinates (labeled "LR").

Example 7-5. Classification with k-means cluster features

```
>>> from sklearn.linear_model import LogisticRegression
>>> from sklearn.svm import SVC
>>> from sklearn.neighbors import KNeighborsClassifier
>>> from sklearn.ensemble import RandomForestClassifier, GradientBoostingClassifier

### Generate some test data from the same distribution as training data
>>> test_data, test_labels = make_moons(n_samples=2000, noise=0.3)

### Use the k-means featurizer to generate cluster features
>>> training_cluster_features = kmf_hint.transform(training_data)
>>> test_cluster_features = kmf_hint.transform(test_data)
```

```
### Form new input features with cluster features
>>> training_with_cluster = scipy.sparse.hstack((training_data,
...                                               training_cluster_features))
>>> test_with_cluster = scipy.sparse.hstack((test_data, test_cluster_features))

### Build the classifiers
>>> lr_cluster = LogisticRegression(random_state=seed).fit(training_with_cluster,
...                                                         training_labels)
>>> classifier_names = ['LR',
...                     'kNN',
...                     'RBF SVM',
...                     'Random Forest',
...                     'Boosted Trees']
>>> classifiers = [LogisticRegression(random_state=seed),
...                KNeighborsClassifier(5),
...                SVC(gamma=2, C=1),
...                RandomForestClassifier(max_depth=5, n_estimators=10, max_features=1),
...                GradientBoostingClassifier(n_estimators=10, learning_rate=1.0,
...                                           max_depth=5)]
>>> for model in classifiers:
...     model.fit(training_data, training_labels)

### Helper function to evaluate classifier performance using ROC
>>> def test_roc(model, data, labels):
...     if hasattr(model, "decision_function"):
...         predictions = model.decision_function(data)
...     else:
...         predictions = model.predict_proba(data)[:,1]
...     fpr, tpr, _ = sklearn.metrics.roc_curve(labels, predictions)
...     return fpr, tpr

### Plot results
>>> import matplotlib.pyplot as plt
>>> plt.figure()
>>> fpr_cluster, tpr_cluster = test_roc(lr_cluster, test_with_cluster, test_labels)
>>> plt.plot(fpr_cluster, tpr_cluster, 'r-', label='LR with k-means')

>>> for i, model in enumerate(classifiers):
...     fpr, tpr = test_roc(model, test_data, test_labels)
...     plt.plot(fpr, tpr, label=classifier_names[i])

>>> plt.plot([0, 1], [0, 1], 'k--')
>>> plt.legend()
```

Figure 7-7 shows the receiver operating characteristic (ROC) curves of each of the classifiers when evaluated on the test set. A ROC curve shows the trade-off between true positives and false positives as we vary the classification decision boundary. (See Zheng [2015] for more details.) A good classifier should quickly reach a high true positive rate and a low false positive rate, so curves that rise sharply toward the upper-left corner are good.

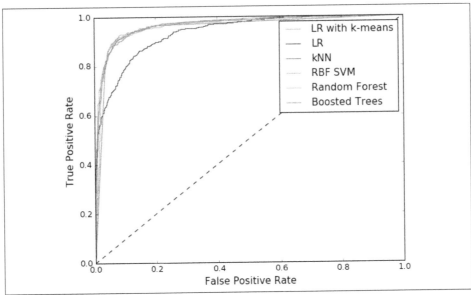

Figure 7-7. ROCs of k-means + logistic regression versus nonlinear classifiers and plain logistic regression on the synthetic two-moons dataset

Our plot shows that logistic regression performs much better with cluster features than without. In fact, with cluster features, the linear classifier performs just as well as nonlinear classifiers. One minor caveat is that in this toy example, we did not tune the hyperparameters for any of the models. There may be performance differences once the models are fully tuned, but at least this shows that it is possible for LR with k-means to be on a par with nonlinear classifiers. This is a nice result because linear classifiers are much cheaper to train than nonlinear classifiers. Lower computation cost allows us to try more models with different features in the same period of time, which increases the chance of ending up with a much better model.

Alternative Dense Featurization

Instead of one-hot cluster membership, a data point can also be represented by a dense vector of its inverse distance to each cluster center. This retains more information than simple binary cluster assignment, but the representation is now dense. There is a trade-off here. One-hot cluster membership results in a very lightweight, sparse representation, but one might need a larger k to represent data of complex shapes. Inverse distance representation is dense, which could be more expensive for the modeling step, but one might be able to get away with a smaller k.

A compromise between sparse and dense is to retain inverse distances for only p of the closest clusters. But now p is an extra hyperparameter to tune. (Can you understand why feature engineering requires so much fiddling?) There is no free lunch.

Pros, Cons, and Gotchas

Using k-means to turn spatial data into features is an example of *model stacking*, where the input to one model is the output of another. Another example of stacking is to use the output of a decision tree–type model (random forest or gradient boosting tree) as input to a linear classifier. Stacking has become an increasingly popular technique in recent years. Nonlinear classifiers are expensive to train and maintain. The key intuition with stacking is to push the nonlinearities into the features and use a very simple, usually linear model as the last layer. The featurizer can be trained offline, which means that one can use expensive models that require more computation power or memory but generate useful features. The simple model at the top level can be quickly adapted to the changing distributions of online data. This is a great trade-off between accuracy and speed, and this strategy is often used in applications like targeted advertising that require fast adaptation to changing data distributions.

Key Intuition for Model Stacking

Use sophisticated base layers (often with expensive models) to generate good (often nonlinear) features, combined with a simple and fast top-layer model. This often strikes the right balance between model accuracy and speed.

Compared to using a nonlinear classifier, k-means stacked with logistic regression is cheaper to train and store. Table 7-1 is a chart detailing the training and prediction complexity in both computation and memory for a number of machine learning models. n denotes the number of data points, d the number of (original) features.

Table 7-1. Complexity of ML models

Model	Time	Space
k-means training	$O(nkd)$[a]	$O(kd)$
k-means predict	$O(kd)$	$O(kd)$
LR + cluster features training	$O(n(d+k))$	$O(d+k)$
LR + cluster features predict	$O(d+k)$	$O(d+k)$
RBF SVM training	$O(n^2d)$	$O(n^2)$
RBF SVM predict	$O(sd)$	$O(sd)$
GBT training	$O(nd2^mt)$	$O(nd + 2^mt)$
GBT predict	$O(2^mt)$	$O(2^mt)$
kNN training	$O(1)$	$O(nd)$
kNN predict	$O(nd + k \log n)$	$O(nd)$

[a] Streaming k-means can be done in time $O(nd (\log k + \log \log n))$, which is much faster than $O(nkd)$ for large k.

For k-means, the training time is $O(nkd)$ because each iteration involves computing the d-dimensional distance between every data point and every centroid (k). We optimistically assume that the number of iterations is not a function of n, though this may not be true in all cases. Prediction requires computing the distance between the new data point and each of the k centroids, which is $O(kd)$. The storage space requirement is $O(kd)$, for the coordinates of the k centroids.

Logistic regression training and prediction are linear in both the number of data points and feature dimensions. RBF SVM training is expensive because it involves computing the kernel matrix for every pair of input data. RBF SVM prediction is less expensive than training; it is linear in the number of support vectors s and the feature dimension d. GBT training and prediction are linear in data size and the size of the model (t trees, each with at most 2^m leaves, where m is the maximum depth of the tree). A naive implementation of kNN requires no training time at all because the training data itself is essentially the model. The cost is paid at prediction time, where the input must be evaluated against each of the original training points and partially sorted to retrieve the k closest neighbors.

Overall, k-means + LR is the only combination that is linear (with respect to the size of training data, $O(nd)$, and model size, $O(kd)$) at both training and prediction time. The complexity is most similar to that of GBT, which has costs that are linear in the number of data points, the feature dimension, and the size of the model ($O(2^m t)$). It is hard to say whether k-means + LR or GBT will result in a smaller model—it depends on the spatial characteristics of the data.

Potential for Data Leakage

Those who remember our caution regarding data leakage (see "Guarding against data leakage" on page 93) might ask whether including the target variable in the k-means featurization step would cause such a problem. The answer is "yes," but not as much in the case of bin counting. If we use the same dataset for learning the clusters and building the classification model, then information about the target will have leaked into the input variables. As a result, accuracy evaluations *on the training data* will probably be overly optimistic, but the bias will go away when evaluating on a hold-out validation set or test set. Furthermore, the leakage will not be as bad as in the case of bin-counting statistics (see "Bin Counting" on page 87), because the lossy compression of the clustering algorithm will have abstracted away some of that information. To be extra careful about preventing leakage, hold out a separate dataset for deriving the clusters, just like in the case of bin counting.

k-means featurization is useful for real-valued, bounded numeric features that form clumps of dense regions in space. The clumps can be of any shape, because we can just increase the number of clusters to approximate them. (Unlike in the classic clustering setup, we are not concerned with discovering the "true" number of clusters; we only need to cover them.)

k-means cannot handle feature spaces where the Euclidean distance does not make sense—i.e., weirdly distributed numeric variables or categorical variables. If the feature set contains those variables, then there are several ways to handle them:

1. Apply k-means featurization only on the real-valued, bounded numeric features.
2. Define a custom metric to handle multiple data types and use the k-medoids algorithms. (k-medoids is analogous to k-means but allows for arbitrary distance metrics.)
3. Convert categorical variables to binning statistics (see "Bin Counting" on page 87), then featurize them using k-means.

Combined with techniques for handling categorical variables and time series, k-means featurization can be adapted to handle the kind of rich data that often appears in customer marketing and sales analytics. The resulting clusters can be thought of as user segments, which are very useful features for the next modeling step.

Summary

This chapter illustrated the concept of model stacking using a somewhat unconventional approach: combining supervised k-means with a simple linear classifier. k-means is usually used as an unsupervised modeling method to find dense clusters of data points in feature space. Here, however, k-means is optionally given the class labels as input. This helps k-means to find clusters that better align with the boundary between classes.

Deep learning, which we will discuss in the next chapter, takes model stacking to a whole new level by layering neural networks on top of one another. Two recent winners of the ImageNet Large Scale Visual Recognition Challenge involved 13 and 22 layers of neural networks. They take advantage of the availability of lots of unlabeled training images and look for combinations of pixels that yield good image features. The technique in this chapter separately trains the k-means featurizer from the linear classifier. But it's possible to jointly optimize the featurizer and the classier. As we shall see, deep learning training takes the latter route.

Bibliography

Dunning, Ted. The man is a walking encyclopedia of data science. He is a frequent speaker at industry events, and likes beer and nice people. Buy him a beer and talk to him. You won't regret it.

Zheng, Alice. *Evaluating Machine Learning Models* (*http://www.oreilly.com/data/free/ evaluating-machine-learning-models.csp*). Sebastopol, CA: O'Reilly Media, 2015.

## CHAPTER 8

Automating the Featurizer: Image Feature Extraction and Deep Learning

Sight and sound are innate sensory inputs for humans. Our brains are hardwired to rapidly evolve our abilities to process visual and auditory signals, with some systems developing to respond to stimulus even before birth (Eliot, 2000). Language skills, on the other hand, are learned. They take months to develop and years to master. Many people take the development of their vision and hearing for granted, but all of us have had to intentionally train our brains to understand and use language.

Interestingly, the situation is the reverse for machine learning. We have made much more headway with text analysis applications than image or audio. Take the problem of search, for example. People have enjoyed years of relative success in information retrieval and text search, whereas image and audio search are still being perfected (though the breakthrough in deep learning models in the last five years may finally herald the long-awaited revolution in image and speech analysis).

The difficulty of progress is directly related to the difficulty of extracting meaningful features from the respective types of data. Machine learning models require semantically meaningful features to make semantically meaningful predictions. In text analysis, particularly for languages such as English where a basic unit of semantic meaning (a word) is easily extractable, progress can be made very fast. Images and audio, on the other hand, are recorded as digital pixels or waveforms. A single "atom" in an image is a pixel. In audio data, it is a single measurement of waveform intensity. These contain much less semantic information than an atom—a word—of text data. Therefore, the job of feature extraction and engineering is much more challenging on image and audio than on text.

In the last 20 years, computer vision research has focused on manually defined pipelines for extracting good image features. For a while, image feature extractors such as

SIFT and HOG (described in the following sections) were the standard. Recent developments in deep learning research have extended the reach of traditional machine learning models by incorporating automatic feature extraction in the base layers. They essentially replace manually defined feature image extractors with manually defined models that automatically learn and extract features. The manual work is still there, just abstracted further into the belly of the modeling beast.

In this chapter, we will start with the most popular image feature extractors and then dive into the most complicated modeling machinery covered in this book: deep learning for feature learning.

The Simplest Image Features (and Why They Don't Work)

What are the *right* features to extract from an image? The answer of course depends on what we are trying to do with those features. Let's say our task is image retrieval: we are given a picture and asked to find similar pictures from a database of images. We need to decide how to represent each image, and how to measure the differences between them. Can we just look at the percentage of different colors in an image? Figure 8-1 shows two pictures having roughly the same color profile but very different meanings; one looks like white cloud in a blue sky, and the other is the flag of Greece. So, color information is probably not enough to characterize an image.

Figure 8-1. Blue and white pictures—same color profile, very different meanings

Another simple idea is to measure the pixel value differences between images. First, resize the images to have the same width and height. Each image is represented by a matrix of pixel values. The matrix can be stacked into one long vector, either by row or by column. The color of each pixel (e.g., the RGB encoding of the color) is now a feature of the image. Finally, measure the Euclidean distance between the long pixel vectors. This would definitely allow us to tell apart the Greek flag and the white clouds, but it is too stringent as a similarity measure. A cloud could take on a thousand different shapes and still be a cloud. It could be shifted to the side of the image, or half of it might lie in shadow. All of these transformations would increase the

Euclidean distance, but they shouldn't change the fact that the picture is still of a cloud.

The problem is that individual pixels do not carry enough semantic information about the image. Therefore, they are bad atomic units for analysis.

Manual Feature Extraction: SIFT and HOG

In 1999, computer vision researchers figured out a better way to represent images using statistics of image patches: the *Scale Invariant Feature Transform* (SIFT) [Lowe, 1999].

SIFT was originally developed for the task of object recognition, which involves not only correctly tagging the image as containing an object, but pinpointing its location in the image. The process involves analyzing the image at a pyramid of possible scales, detecting interest points that could indicate the presence of the object, extracting features (commonly called *image descriptors* in computer vision) about the interest points, and determining the pose of the object.

Over the years, the usage of SIFT expanded to extract features not only for interest points but across the entire image. The SIFT feature extraction procedure is very similar to another technique, called the Histogram of Oriented Gradients (HOG) [Dalal and Triggs, 2005]. Both of them essentially compute histograms of gradient orientations. We now describe this process in detail.

Image Gradients

To do better than raw pixel values, we have to somehow "organize" the pixels into more informative units. Differences between neighboring pixels are often very useful. Pixel values usually differ at the boundary of objects, when there is a shadow, within a pattern, or on a textured surface. The difference in value between neighboring pixels is called an *image gradient*.

The simplest way to compute the image gradient is to separately calculate the differences along the horizontal (x) and vertical (y) axes of the image, then compose them into a 2D vector. This involves two 1D difference operations that can be handily represented by a vector mask or filter. The mask [1, 0, –1] takes the difference between the left neighbor and the right neighbor or the up-neighbor and the down-neighbor, depending on which direction we apply the mask. There are 2D gradient filters as well, but for the purpose of this example, the 1D filter suffices.

To apply a filter to an image, we perform a *convolution*. It involves flipping the filter and taking the inner product with a small patch of the image, then moving to the next patch. Convolutions are very common in signal processing. We'll use * to denote the operation:

$$[a\ b\ c] * [1\ 2\ 3] = c*1 + b*2 + a*3$$

The x and y gradients at pixel (i,j) are:

$$g_x(i,j) = [1\ 0\ -1] * [I(i-1,j)\ I(i,j)\ I(i+1,j)] = -1 * I(i-1,j) + 1 * I(i+1,j)$$

$$g_y(i,j) = [1\ 0\ -1] * [I(i,j-1)\ I(i,j)\ I(i,j+1)] = -1 * I(i,j-1) + 1 * I(i,j+1)$$

Together, they form the gradient:

$$\nabla I(i,\ j) = \begin{bmatrix} g_x(i,\ j) \\ g_y(i,\ j) \end{bmatrix}$$

A vector can be completely described by its direction and magnitude. The magnitude of the gradient is equal to the Euclidean norm of the gradient $\left(\sqrt{g_x^2 + g_y^2}\right)$, which indicates how much the pixel values change around the pixel. The direction or orientation of the gradient depends on the relative size of the change in the horizontal and vertical directions; it can be computed as $\theta = \arctan\left(\frac{g_y}{g_x}\right)$. Figure 8-2 illustrates these mathematical concepts.

Figure 8-3 illustrates examples of the simple image gradient that is composed of the vertical and horizontal gradients. Each example is an image of nine pixels. Each pixel is labeled with a grayscale value. (Smaller numbers correspond to a darker color.) The gradient for the center pixel is shown below each image. The image on the left contains horizontal stripes, where the color only changes vertically. Therefore, the horizontal gradient is zero and the gradient is nonzero vertically. The center image contains vertical stripes; therefore, the horizontal gradient is zero. The image on the right contains diagonal stripes and the gradient is also diagonal.

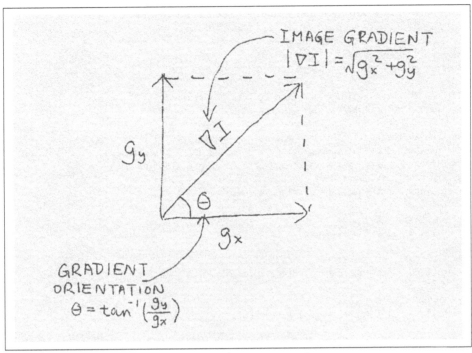

Figure 8-2. Illustration of the definition of an image gradient

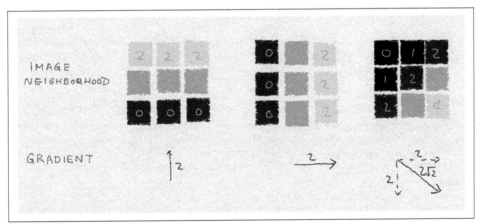

Figure 8-3. Simple examples of the image gradient

The definition works on synthetic toy examples. But would it work well on a real image? In Example 8-1, we examine this using a picture of a cat from `scikit-image` (*http://scikit-image.org/*), shown in Figure 8-4 with its horizontal and vertical gradients. Since the gradients are computed at every pixel location of the original image, we end up with two new matrices, each of which can be visualized as an image.

Example 8-1. Calculating simple image gradients using Python

```
>>> import matplotlib.pyplot as plt
>>> import numpy as np
>>> from skimage import data, color

### Load the example image and turn it into grayscale
>>> image = color.rgb2gray(data.chelsea())

### Compute the horizontal gradient using the centered 1D filter.
### This is equivalent to replacing each non-border pixel with the
### difference between its right and left neighbors. The leftmost
### and rightmost edges have a gradient of 0.
>>> gx = np.empty(image.shape, dtype=np.double)
>>> gx[:, 0] = 0
>>> gx[:, -1] = 0
>>> gx[:, 1:-1] = image[:, :-2] - image[:, 2:]

### Same deal for the vertical gradient
>>> gy = np.empty(image.shape, dtype=np.double)
>>> gy[0, :] = 0
>>> gy[-1, :] = 0
>>> gy[1:-1, :] = image[:-2, :] - image[2:, :]

### Matplotlib incantations
>>> fig, (ax1, ax2, ax3) = plt.subplots(3, 1,
...                                     figsize=(5, 9),
...                                     sharex=True,
...                                     sharey=True)

>>> ax1.axis('off')
>>> ax1.imshow(image, cmap=plt.cm.gray)
>>> ax1.set_title('Original image')
>>> ax1.set_adjustable('box-forced')

>>> ax2.axis('off')
>>> ax2.imshow(gx, cmap=plt.cm.gray)
>>> ax2.set_title('Horizontal gradients')
>>> ax2.set_adjustable('box-forced')

>>> ax3.axis('off')
>>> ax3.imshow(gy, cmap=plt.cm.gray)
>>> ax3.set_title('Vertical gradients')
>>> ax3.set_adjustable('box-forced')
```

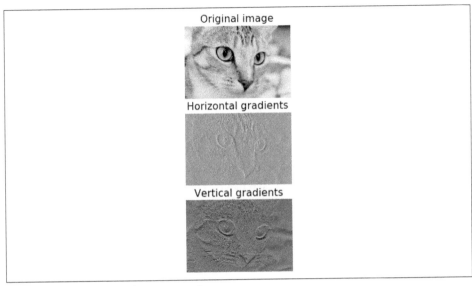

Figure 8-4. Gradients of an image of a cat

Note that the horizontal gradient picks out strong *vertical* patterns such as the inner edges of the cat's eyes, while the vertical gradient picks out strong *horizontal* patterns such as the whiskers and the upper and lower lids of the eyes. This might seem a little paradoxical at first, but it makes sense once we think about it a bit more. The horizontal (x) gradient identifies changes in the horizontal direction. A strong vertical pattern spans multiple y pixels at roughly the same x position. Hence, vertical patterns result in horizontal differences in pixel values. This is what our eyes detect as well.

Gradient Orientation Histograms

Individual image gradients can pick out minute differences in an image neighborhood. But our eyes see bigger patterns than that. For instance, we see an entire cat's whisker, not just a small section. The human vision system identifies contiguous patterns in a region, so we still have more work to do to summarize the image gradients in a neighborhood.

How exactly might we summarize vectors? A statistician would answer, "Look at the distribution!" SIFT and HOG both take this path. In particular, they compute (normalized) histograms of the gradient vectors as image features. A histogram divides data into bins and counts how many data points are in each bin; this is an (unnormalized) empirical distribution. Normalization ensures that the counts sum to 1. The mathematical language is that it has unit ℓ^1 norm.

An image gradient is a vector, and vectors can be represented by two components: the orientation and magnitude. So, we still need to decide how to design the histogram to take both components into account. SIFT and HOG settled on a scheme where the image gradients are binned by their orientation angle θ, weighted by the magnitude of each gradient. Here is the procedure:

1. Divide 0°–360° into equal-sized bins.

2. For each pixel in the neighborhood, add a weight w to the bin corresponding to its orientation θ. w is a function of the magnitude of the gradient and other relevant information. For instance, that information might be the inverse distance of the pixel to the center of the image patch. The idea is that the weight should be large if the gradient is large, and pixels near the center of the image neighborhood matter more than pixels that are farther away.

3. Normalize the histogram.

Figure 8-5 provides an illustration of a gradient orientation histogram of 8 bins composed from an image neighborhood of 4 × 4 pixels.

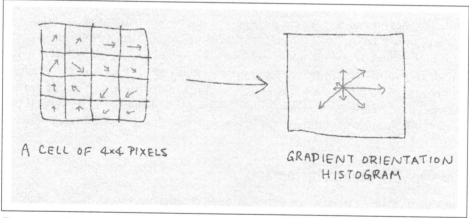

Figure 8-5. Illustration of a gradient orientation histogram of 8 bins based on gradients from a 4 × 4 square cell of pixels

There are, of course, a number of knobs to tweak in the basic gradient orientation histogram algorithm, as well as some optional bells and whistles. As usual, the right settings are probably highly dependent on the particular images one wants to analyze.

Let's examine next some of the decisions to make and the effects these can have on your model.

How many bins should there be? Should they span from 0°–360° (signed gradients) or 0°–180° (unsigned gradients)?

Having more bins leads to finer-grained quantization of gradient orientation, and thus retains more information about the original gradients. But having too many bins is unnecessary and could lead to overfitting to the training data. For example, recognizing a cat in an image probably does not depend on the cat's whisker being oriented exactly at 3°.

There is also the question of whether the bins should span from 0°–360°, which would retain the sign of the gradient along the y-axis, or from 0°–180°, which would not retain the sign of the vertical gradient. The authors of the original HOG paper (Dalal and Triggs, 2005) experimentally determined that 9 bins spanning from 0°–180° is best, whereas the SIFT paper (Lowe, 2004) recommended 8 bins spanning from 0°–360°.

What weight functions should be used?

The HOG paper compares various gradient magnitude weighting schemes: the magnitude itself, its square or square root, binarized, or clipped at the high or low ends. The plain magnitude, without adornments, performed the best in the authors' experiments.

SIFT also uses the plain magnitude of the gradient. Additionally, it wants to avoid sudden changes in the feature descriptor resulting from small changes in the position of the image window, so it downweights gradients that come from the edges of the neighborhood using a Gaussian distance function measured from the window center. In other words, the gradient magnitude is multiplied by $\frac{1}{2\pi\sigma^2}e^{-\|p-p_0\|^2/2\sigma^2}$, where p is the location of the pixel that generated the gradient, p_0 is the location of the center of the image neighborhood, and σ, the width of the Gaussian, is set to one-half the radius of the neighborhood.

SIFT also wants to avoid large changes in the orientation histogram resulting from small changes in the orientation of individual image gradients. So, it uses an interpolation trick that spreads the weight from a single gradient into adjacent orientation bins. In particular, the root bin (the bin that the gradient is assigned to) gets a vote of 1 times the weighted magnitude. Each of the adjacent bins get a vote of $1 - d$, where d is the difference in histogram bin unit from the root bin.

Overall, the vote from a single image gradient for SIFT is:

$$w_{(\nabla p, b)} = w_b \sigma \, \| \, \nabla_p \, \|$$

where ∇_p is the gradient of pixel p in bin b, w_b is the interpolation weight of b, and σ is the Gaussian distance to the center from p.

How are neighborhoods defined? How should they cover the image?

HOG and SIFT both settled on a two-level representation of image neighborhoods: first adjacent pixels are organized into cells, and neighboring cells are then organized into blocks. An orientation histogram is computed for each cell, and the cell histogram vectors are concatenated to form the final feature descriptor for the whole block.

SIFT uses cells of 16×16 pixels, organized into 8 orientation bins, then grouped by blocks of 4×4 cells, making for $4 \times 4 \times 8 = 128$ features for the image neighborhood.

The HOG paper experimented with rectangular and circular shapes for the cells and blocks. Rectangular cells are called R-HOG blocks. The best R-HOG setting was found to be 8×8 pixels with 9 orientation bins each, grouped into blocks of 2×2 cells. Circular cells are called C-HOG blocks, with variants determined by the radius of the central cell, whether or not the cells are radially divided, the width of the outer cells, etc.

No matter how the neighborhoods are organized, they typically overlap to form the feature vector for the whole image. In other words, cells and blocks shift across the image horizontally and vertically, a few pixels at a time, to cover the entire image.

The main ingredients of neighborhood architecture are multilevel organization and overlapping windows that shift across the image. The same ingredients are utilized in the design of deep learning networks.

What kind of normalization should be done?

Normalization evens out the feature descriptors so that they have comparable magnitude. It is synonymous with scaling, which we discussed in Chapter 4. We found that feature scaling on text features (in the form of tf-idf) did not have a large effect on classification accuracy. The story is quite different for image features, which can be quite sensitive to changes in lighting and contrast that appear in natural images. For instance, consider images of an apple under a strong spotlight versus a soft diffused light coming through a window. The image gradients would have very different magnitudes, even though the object is the same. For this reason, image featurization in computer vision usually starts with global color normalization to remove illumination and contrast variance. For SIFT and HOG, it turns out that such preprocessing is unnecessary so long as we normalize the features.

SIFT follows a normalize–threshold–normalize scheme. First, the block feature vector is normalized to unit length (ℓ^2 normalization). Then, the features are clipped to a maximum value in order to get rid of extreme lighting effects such as color saturation from the camera. Finally, the clipped features are again normalized to unit length.

The HOG paper experimented with different normalization schemes involving ℓ^2 and ℓ^1 norms, including the normalize–threshold–normalize scheme used in the SIFT paper. The authors found pure ℓ^1 normalization to be slightly less reliable than the other methods (which performed comparably).

SIFT Architecture

The SIFT pipeline requires quite a number of steps. HOG is slightly simpler but follows many of the same basic steps, such as creating a gradient histogram and normalization. Figure 8-6 illustrates the SIFT architecture. Starting from a region of interest in the original image, we first divide the region into a grid. Each grid cell is then further divided into subgrids. Each subgrid element contains a number of pixels, and each pixel produces a gradient. Each subgrid element produces a weighted gradient estimate, where the weights are chosen so that gradients outside of the subgrid element can contribute. These gradient estimates are then aggregated into an orientation histogram for the subgrid, where gradients can have weighted votes as described previously. The orientation histograms for each subgrid are then concatenated to form a long gradient orientation histogram for the entire grid. (If the grid is divided into 2 × 2 subgrids, then there will be 4 gradient orientation histograms to concatenate into 1.) This is the feature vector for the grid, which then goes through a normalize–threshold–normalize process. First, the vector is normalized to have unit norm. Then, individual values are clipped to a maximum threshold. Finally, the thresholded vector is normalized again. This is the final SIFT feature descriptor for the image patch.

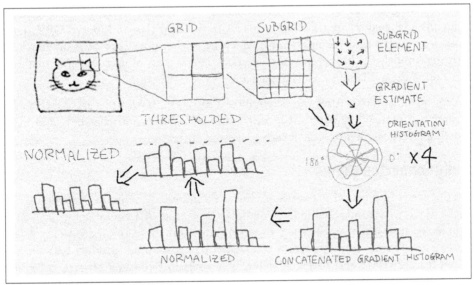

Figure 8-6. SIFT architecture—steps to produce a feature vector for a region of interest in the original image

Learning Image Features with Deep Neural Networks

SIFT and HOG went a long way toward defining good image features. However, the latest gains in computer vision have come from a very different direction: deep neural network models. The breakthrough happened at the ImageNet Large Scale Visual Recognition Challenge (ILSVRC) in 2012, where a group of researchers from the University of Toronto nearly halved the error rate of the previous year's winner. They branded their method "deep learning" to emphasize that, unlike previous architecture neural network models, the latest generation contains many layers of neural networks and transformations stacked on top of each other. The winning model of ILSVRC 2012—subsequently dubbed AlexNet, after the name of the lead author—has 13 layers (Krizhevsky et al., 2012). The winner of ILSVRC 2014, GoogLeNet, has 22 layers (Szegedy et al., 2014).

On the surface, the mechanism of stacked neural networks appears very different from the image gradient histograms of SIFT and HOG. But a visualization of AlexNet shows that the first few layers are essentially computing edge gradients and other simple patterns, much like SIFT and HOG. Subsequent layers combine local patterns into more global patterns. The end result is a feature extractor that is much more powerful than what came before.

The infrastructure of stacked layers of neural networks (or any other classification model) is not new. But training such complex models requires a lot of data and a lot of computing power, which was not available until recently. The ImageNet dataset contains a labeled set of 1.2 million images from 1,000 classes. Modern GPUs have sped up matrix-vector computations, which lie at the inner core of many machine learning models (including neural networks). The success of deep learning methods rests upon the availability of lots of data and lots of GPU hours.

Deep learning architectures can be composed of several types of layers. AlexNet, for instance, contains fully connected, convolutional response normalization, and max-pooling layers. We'll now look at each of these in turn.

Fully Connected Layers

At the core of all neural networks are linear functions of the input. Logistic regression, which we encountered in Chapter 4, is an example of a neural network. A fully connected neural network is simply a set of linear functions of all of the input features. Recall that a linear function can be written as an inner product between the input feature vector and a weight vector, plus a possible constant term. A collection of linear functions can be represented as a matrix-vector product, where the weight vector becomes a weight matrix (W).

The mathematical definition of a fully connected layer is:

$$z = \mathbf{W}\mathbf{x} + \mathbf{b}$$

where each row of $\mathbf{W}$ is a weight vector that maps the entire input vector x into a single output in z. b is a vector of scalars representing the constant offset (or bias) for each neuron.

The fully connected layer is so named because every input can be used in every output. Mathematically, this means that there are no restrictions on the values in the matrix $\mathbf{W}$. (As we will soon see, a convolutional layer makes use of only a small subset of inputs for each output.) Pictorially, a fully connected neural net can be represented by a complete bipartite graph where every node in the input is connected to every node in the output (see Figure 8-7).

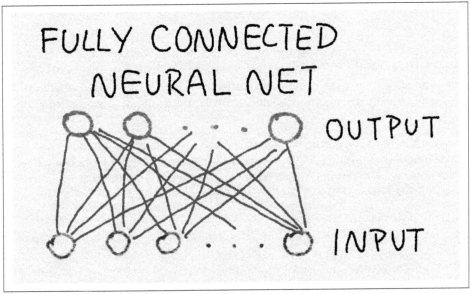

Figure 8-7. A fully connected neural network, represented as a graph

Fully connected layers contain the maximum possible number of parameters (#input × #output)—hence, they are considered expensive. Such dense connection allows the network to detect global patterns that could involve all inputs. The last two layers of AlexNet are fully connected for this reason. The outputs are still independent from each other, conditioned on the inputs.

Convolutional Layers

In contrast to fully connected layers, a convolutional layer uses only a subset of inputs for each output. The transformation "moves" across the input, producing outputs using a few features at a time. For simplicity, one can use the same weights for different sets of input, instead of learning new weights for each set of input.

Mathematically, the convolution operator takes two functions as input and produces one function as output. It flips one of the input functions, moves it across the other function, and outputs the total area under the multiplied curves at each point:

$$(f * g)(t) = \int_{-\infty}^{\infty} f(\tau)g(t - \tau)d\tau = \int_{-\infty}^{\infty} g(\tau)f(t - \tau)d\tau$$

The way to compute total area under a curve is to take its integral. The operator is symmetric in the inputs, meaning that it does not matter whether we flip the first input or the second; the output is the same.

We've already seen an example of simple convolution, when we looked at image gradients ("Image Gradients" on page 135). But the mathematical definition of convolution may still appear to be somewhat convoluted. There is reason to its madness. It's easiest to explain the intuition behind convolution using an example from signal processing.

Imagine that we have a little black box. To see what the black box does, we pass a single unit of stimulus through it. We record whatever the output looks like on a little sheet of paper. We wait until there is no more response to the original stimulus. The resulting function over time is the *response function*; let's call it $g(t)$.

Imagine now that we have some crazy wild signal $f(t)$, which we proceed to feed through the black box. At time $t = 0$, $f(0)$ interacts with the black box and produces $f(0)$ multiplied by $g(0)$. At time $t = 1$, $f(1)$ enters the black box and gets multiplied by $g(0)$. At the same time, the black box continues to respond to the previous signal $f(0)$, which is now multiplied by $g(1)$. So, the total output at time $t = 1$ is $(f(0) * g(1)) + (f(1) * g(0))$. At time $t = 2$, the situation gets even more complicated, with $f(2)$ entering the picture, and $f(0)$ and $f(1)$ continuing to generate their responses. The total output at time $t = 2$ is $(f(0) * g(2)) + (f(1) * g(1)) + (f(2) * g(0))$. In this way, the response function effectively gets flipped in time, with $\tau = 0$ always interacting with whatever is currently entering the black box, and the tail of the response function interacting with whatever came before.

Figure 8-8 illustrates the quantities at play at each time step (note that we've made time discrete for convenience of description—in reality, time is continuous, so the summation is really an integral). When computing the value of the convolution at a particular time step, you multiply the overlapping signals together and sum them.

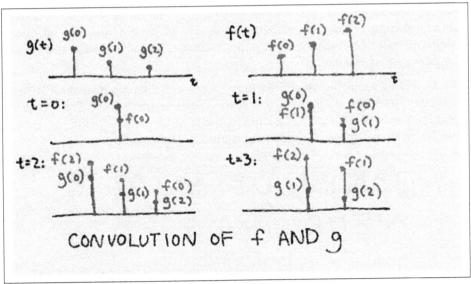

Figure 8-8. Convolution of two discrete signals, f and g

This black box is called a linear system because it doesn't do anything more crazy than scalar multiplication and summation. The convolution operator cleanly captures the effect of a linear system.

Intuition Behind Convolution

The convolution operator captures the effect of a linear system, which multiplies the incoming signal with its response function, summing over current responses to all past input.

In our example, $g(t)$ is used to denote the response function, and $f(t)$ the input. But since convolution is symmetric, it doesn't really matter which is the response and which the input. The output is simply a combination of both. $g(t)$ is also known as a filter.[1]

Images are two-dimensional signals, so we need a 2D filter. A 2D *convolutional filter* extends the 1D case by taking the integral over two variables:

$$(f * g)[i, j] = \sum_{u=0}^{m} \sum_{v=0}^{n} f[u, v]g[i - u, j - v]$$

---

1 Technically, a filter is a transformation that eliminates certain parts of the Fourier spectrum. But it is increasingly common to use "filter" as a generic term.

Since digital images have discrete pixels, the convolution integrals become discrete sums. Furthermore, since the number of pixels is finite, the filter function only needs a finite number of elements. In image processing, a 2D convolutional filter is also known as a *kernel* or a *mask*.

When applying a convolutional filter to an image, one does not necessarily define a giant filter that covers the entire image. Rather, one formulates a small filter covering just a few pixels by a few pixels and applies the same filter across the image, shifting over the horizontal and vertical pixel directions (see Figure 8-9).

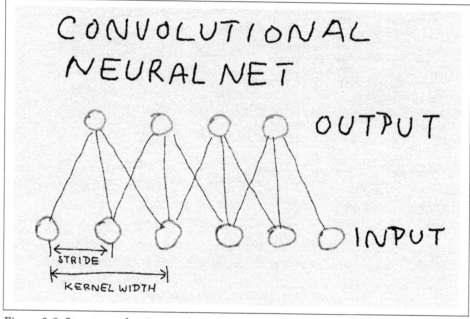

Figure 8-9. Structure of a 1D convolutional neural net

Because the same filter is used across the image, one only needs to define a small set of parameters. The trade-off is that the filter can absorb information only within a small pixel neighborhood at a time. In other words, a convolutional neural net identifies local patterns instead of global ones.

Convolutional Filter Example

In this example, we apply a Gaussian filter to an image. The Gaussian function forms a smooth and symmetric mound around zero. The filter produces a weighted average of nearby function values. When applied to an image, it has the effect of blurring nearby pixel values. The 2D Gaussian filter is defined by:

$$G(x, y) = \frac{1}{2\pi\sigma}e^{-\frac{x^2+y^2}{2\sigma^2}},$$

where σ is the standard deviation of the Gaussian function, which controls the width of the "mound."

In Example 8-2, we'll first create a 2D Gaussian filter, then convolve it with our favorite cat image to produce a blurred cat (see Figure 8-10). Note that this is not the most accurate way to compute a Gaussian filter, but it is the easiest to understand. A better implementation would take the weighted average value at each discrete point rather than the simple point estimate.

Example 8-2. Applying a simple Gaussian filter on an image

```
>>> import numpy as np

# First create X,Y meshgrids of size 5x5 on which we compute the Gaussian
>>> ind = [-1., -0.5, 0., 0.5, 1.]
>>> X,Y = np.meshgrid(ind, ind)
>>> X
array([[-1. , -0.5, 0. , 0.5, 1. ],
       [-1. , -0.5, 0. , 0.5, 1. ],
       [-1. , -0.5, 0. , 0.5, 1. ],
       [-1. , -0.5, 0. , 0.5, 1. ],
       [-1. , -0.5, 0. , 0.5, 1. ]])

# G is a simple, unnormalized Gaussian kernel where the value at (0,0) is 1.0
>>> G = np.exp(-(np.multiply(X,X) + np.multiply(Y,Y))/2)
>>> G
array([[ 0.36787944, 0.53526143, 0.60653066, 0.53526143, 0.36787944],
       [ 0.53526143, 0.77880078, 0.8824969 , 0.77880078, 0.53526143],
       [ 0.60653066, 0.8824969 , 1.        , 0.8824969 , 0.60653066],
       [ 0.53526143, 0.77880078, 0.8824969 , 0.77880078, 0.53526143],
       [ 0.36787944, 0.53526143, 0.60653066, 0.53526143, 0.36787944]])

>>> from skimage import data, color
>>> cat = color.rgb2gray(data.chelsea())

>>> from scipy import signal
>>> blurred_cat = signal.convolve2d(cat, G, mode='valid')

>>> import matplotlib.pyplot as plt
>>> fig, (ax1, ax2) = plt.subplots(1, 2, figsize=(10,4),
...                                sharex=True, sharey=True)

>>> ax1.axis('off')
>>> ax1.imshow(cat, cmap=plt.cm.gray)
>>> ax1.set_title('Input image')
>>> ax1.set_adjustable('box-forced')

>>> ax2.axis('off')
```

```
>>> ax2.imshow(blurred_cat, cmap=plt.cm.gray)
>>> ax2.set_title('After convolving with a Gaussian filter')
>>> ax2.set_adjustable('box-forced')
```

Input image

After convolving with a Gaussian filter

Figure 8-10. An image of a cat, before and after applying a 2D Gaussian filter

The convolutional layers in AlexNet are three-dimensional. In other words they operate on voxels (values in the array representing the 3D space of the image) from the previous layer. The first convolutional neural net takes raw RGB images and learns convolution filters for a local image neighborhood across all three color channels. Subsequent layers take as input voxels across space and kernel dimensions. See Figure 8-14 for more details.

Rectified Linear Unit (ReLU) Transformation

The output of a neural net is often passed through another nonlinear transformation, also known as an *activation function*. Common choices are the *tanh* function (a smooth nonlinear function bounded between –1 and 1), the *sigmoid* function (a smooth nonlinear function bounded between 0 and 1, introduced in "Classification with Logistic Regression" on page 66), or what's known as a *rectified linear unit*. A ReLU is a simple variation of a linear function where the negative part is zeroed out. In other words, it trims away the negative values, but leaves the positive part unbounded. The range of ReLU extends from 0 to ∞.

Common Activation Functions

A ReLU is a linear function with the negative part zeroed out:

$$\text{ReLU}(x) = \max(0, x)$$

The tanh function is a trigonometric function that smoothly increases from –1 to 1:

$$\tanh(x) = \frac{\sinh(x)}{\cosh(x)} = \frac{e^x - e^{-x}}{e^x + e^{-x}}$$

The sigmoid function increases smoothly from 0 to 1:

$$sigmoid(x) = \frac{1}{1 + e^{-x}}$$

The three functions are illustrated in Figure 8-11.

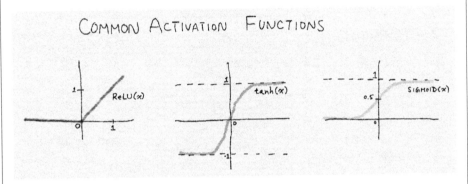

Figure 8-11. Illustration of three common activation functions: ReLU, tanh, and sigmoid

The ReLU transformation has no effect on nonnegative functions such as the raw image or the Gaussian filter. However, a trained neural net, whether fully connected or convolutional, will likely output negative values. AlexNet uses ReLU instead of other transformations, citing faster convergence during training (Krizhevsky et al., 2012). It applies ReLU to every convolutional and fully connected layer.

Response Normalization Layers

After the discussions in Chapter 4 and earlier in this chapter, normalization should by now be a familiar concept. Normalization divides an individual output by a function of the collective total response. Hence, another way of understanding normalization is that it creates competition amongst neighbors because the strength of each output is now measured relative to its neighbors (see Figure 8-12). AlexNet normalizes the output at each location across different kernels.

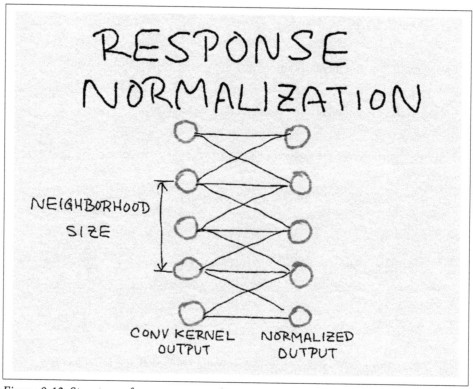

Figure 8-12. Structure of response normalization over convolution kernel outputs from the previous layer—the normalization constants are computed based on a neighborhood from the previous layer

Local Response Normalization Breeds Competition Among Neighboring Kernels

As the name suggests, local response normalization divides a value by a combination of its neighbors. Here is the formula:

$$y_k = x_k \Big/ \Big(c + \alpha \textstyle\sum_{\ell \in \text{neighborhood of } k} x_\ell^2\Big)^\beta$$

Here, x_k is the output of the kth kernel, and y_k is the normalized response relative to other kernels in the neighborhood. The normalization is performed separately for each output location. That is, for each output location (i,j), we normalize across the nearby convolution kernel outputs. Note that this isn't the same as normalizing over the image neighborhood or output locations. The size of the kernel neighborhood, c, α, and β are all hyperparameters that are tuned via a validation set of images.

Pooling Layers

A pooling layer combines multiple inputs into a single output. As the convolutional filter moves across an image, it generates an output for every neighborhood under its lens. Pooling forces a local image neighborhood to produce one value instead of many. This reduces the number of outputs in the intermediate layers of the deep learning network, which effectively reduces the probability of overfitting the network to training data.

There are multiple ways to pool inputs: averaging, summing (or computing a generalized norm), or taking the maximum value. Pooling moves across the image or intermediate output layers. AlexNet uses overlapping max pooling, moving across the image in strides of two pixels (or outputs) and pooling across three neighbors.

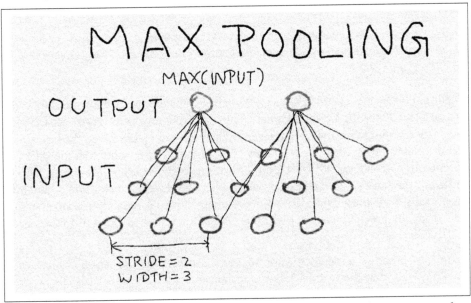

Figure 8-13. Max pooling outputs the maximum number of nonoverlapping rectangles per subregion using nonlinear downsampling

Structure of AlexNet

All together, AlexNet involves five convolution layers, two response normalization layers, three max pooling layers, and two fully connected layers. Combined with the final classification output layer, there are a total of 13 neural network layers in the model, forming 8 layer groups. See Figure 8-14 for details.

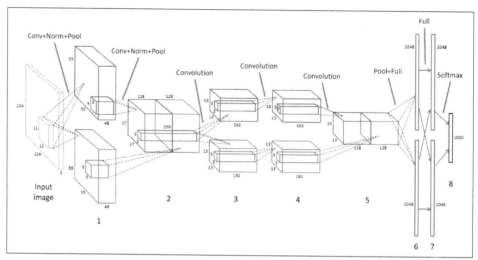

Figure 8-14. Architecture diagram of AlexNet—the different shades of gray (or magenta and blue, if you're viewing the illustrations in color) denote layers that reside on GPU 1 and GPU 2

The input image is first scaled to 256 × 256 pixels. The input is actually random crops of size 224 × 224, with 3 color channels. The first two convolution layers are each followed by a response normalization layer and a max pooling layer, and the last convolution layer is followed by max pooling. The original paper splits training data and computation across two GPUs. Communications between layers are mostly limited to within the same GPU. The exceptions are between layer groups 2 and 3, and after layer group 5. At those boundary points, the next layer takes as input a voxel of kernels from the previous layer across both GPUs. ReLU transformation follows every intermediate layer.

Figure 8-15 shows a detailed view of convolution+response normalization+max pooling. Note that the normalization constant is computed across kernels, whereas pooling happens across image regions. Also, pooling reduces the dimension of the layer.

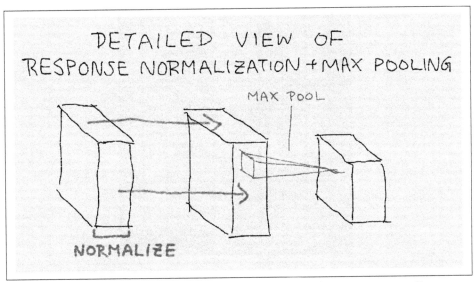

Figure 8-15. Detailed view of convolution+response normalization+max pooling

Note that AlexNet's architecture is reminiscent of the gradient histogram–normalize–threshold–normalize architecture of SIFT/HOG feature extractors (see Figure 8-6), but with many more layers. (Hence the "deep" in "deep learning.") Unlike in SIFT/HOG, however, the convolution kernels and full connection weights are learned from data, not predefined. Also, the normalization steps in SIFT are performed across the feature vector over the entire image region, whereas the response normalization layer in AlexNet normalizes across the convolution kernels.

At a high level, the model starts by extracting patterns out of local image neighborhoods. Each subsequent layer builds upon the output of the previous layers, effectively covering successively larger areas of the original image. Hence, even though the first five convolution layers all have fairly small kernel widths, the later layers are able to formulate more global patterns. The fully connected layers at the end are the most global.

Although the gist of patterns is conceptually clear, it is a hard problem to visualize the actual patterns each layer picks out. Figures 8-16 and 8-17 show visualizations of the first two layers of convolution kernels learned by the model. The first layer consists of detectors of grayscale edges and textures at different orientations, and color blobs and textures. The second layer appears to contain detectors of various smooth patterns.

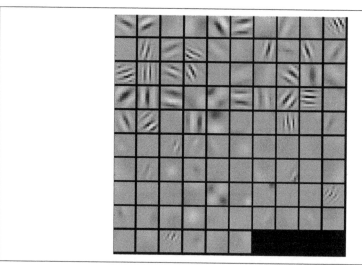

Figure 8-16. Visualization of the first layer of convolution kernels in a trained AlexNet: the first half of the kernels are learned on GPU 1 and appear to detect grayscale edges and textures at different orientations; the second half, trained on a second GPU, focus on color blobs and patterns

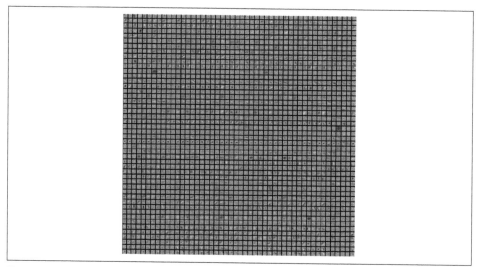

Figure 8-17. Visualization of the second layer of convolution kernels of a trained AlexNet

Despite huge advances in the area, image featurization is still more of an art than a science. Ten years ago, people handcrafted feature extraction steps using a combination of image gradients, edge detection, orientation, spatial cues, smoothing, and normalization. Nowadays, deep learning architects build models that encapsulate much the same ideas, but the parameters are automatically learned from training images. The magic voodoo is still there, just hidden one abstraction deeper in the model!

Summary

Nearing the end, we can build on the intuition gained to better understand why the most straightforward and simple image features will not always be the most useful for performing tasks such as image classification. Instead of representing each pixel as an atomic unit, it is more important to consider the relationships pixels have with other pixels near them. We can adapt techniques developed for other tasks, such as SIFT and HOG, to better extract features across entire images by analyzing gradients in neighborhoods.

The next leap forward in recent years applies deep neural networks to computer vision to push feature extraction of images even further. The important thing to remember here is that deep learning stacks many layers of neural networks and transformations on top of each other. Some of these layers, when examined individually, begin to tease out similar features that can be identified as building blocks for human vision: defining lines, gradients, color maps.

Bibliography

"CS231n: Convolutional Neural Networks for Visual Recognition." Retrieved from *http://cs231n.github.io/convolutional-networks/*.

Dalal, Navneet, and Bill Triggs. "Histograms of Oriented Gradients for Human Detection." *Proceedings of the 2005 IEEE Computer Society Conference on Computer Vision and Pattern Recognition* (2005): 886–893.

Eliot, Lise. *What's Going On in There? How the Brain and Mind Develop in the First Five Years of Life*. New York: Bantam Books, 2000.

Krizhevsky, Alex, Ilya Sutskever, and Geoffrey Hinton. "ImageNet Classification with Deep Convolutional Neural Networks." *Advances in Neural Information Processing Systems* 25 (2012): 1097–1105.

Lowe, David G. "Object Recognition from Local Scale-Invariant Features." *Proceedings of the International Conference on Computer Vision* (1999): 1150–1157.

Lowe, David G. "Distinctive Image Features from Scale-Invariant Keypoints." *International Journal of Computer Vision* 60:2 (2004): 91–110.

Malisiewicz, Tomasz. "From Feature Descriptors to Deep Learning: 20 Years of Computer Vision." Tombone's Computer Vision Blog, January 20, 2015. *http://www.computervisionblog.com/2015/01/from-feature-descriptors-to-deep.html*.

Szegedy, Christian, Wei Liu, Yangqing Jia, Pierre Sermanet, Scott Reed, Dragomir Anguelov, Dumitru Erhan, Vincent Vanhoucke, and Andrew Rabinovich. "Going Deeper with Convolutions." *Proceedings of the 2015 IEEE Conference on Computer Vision and Pattern Recognition* (2015): 1–9.

Zeiler, Matthew D., and Rob Fergus. "Visualizing and Understanding Convolutional Networks," *Proceedings of the 13th European Conference on Computer Vision* (2014): 818–833.

## CHAPTER 9

Back to the Feature: Building an Academic Paper Recommender

"In mathematics you don't understand things. You just get used to them."
—John von Neumann

When the path from data to results was first introduced in Figure 1-1, it may not have been clear how there would ever be a way forward. Throughout this book, we have focused on introducing basic principles of feature engineering using toy models and clean, simple datasets. These examples were intended to be illustrative and enlightening.

Machine learning examples generally show the best-case scenario and results. This masks the path we have described thus far in the book. Now that the foundation is set, we are leaving the world of simple, toy data and diving into the process of feature engineering with a real-world, structured dataset. As we move through each step, we will be examining the raw data forming each feature, what the transformed feature becomes, and what trade-offs we make along the way.

To be clear, our goal for this example is not to build the best model for this dataset. Rather, it is to demonstrate the practical application of a handful of our techniques, as well as how to more deeply examine and understand whether each technique is providing value to the model one is building.

Item-Based Collaborative Filtering

Our task will be to build a recommender for academic papers using a subsample of the Microsoft Academic Graph dataset. This should come in extremely handy for all of you who are searching for citations but have not yet discovered Google Scholar. Here are some relevant statistics about the dataset:

Microsoft Academic Graph Dataset

- It contains 166,192,182 unique papers, available via Open Academic Graph (*https://www.openacademic.ai/oag/*). It is intended to be used for research purposes only.
- The total size of the dataset is 104 GB.
- Each observation has 18 variables to identify each paper, including the paper's title, abstract, authors, keywords, and fields of study.

The dataset is designed to be easy to store and access in a database. It is not tidy for machine learning models out of the box, but requires some initial wrangling. Some teachers like to spare you this step, boosting your ego by getting directly to the models and results. None of that here. We are starting together from the very beginning.

Our initial approach will be to wrangle a few variables into the right shape to push through an item-based collaborative filter. We will see if reasonably similar papers can be found in a timely and efficient manner.

The Origins of Item-Based Collaborative Filtering

This approach was first developed at Amazon as an improvement to user-based algorithms for recommending products. Sarawar et al. (2001) walk through the challenges and benefits of switching the perspective in recommenders from the user to the item.

Item-based collaborative filtering provides recommendations based on the similarity between items. This works in two stages: first finding the similarity scores between items, then ranking all scores to find the top-N similar item recommendations.

Building an Item-Based Recommender

An item-based recommender performs three tasks:

1. Generalize information about a "thing" or item.

2. Score all other items to find ones "like" this one.

3. Return ranked scores + items.

First Pass: Data Import, Cleaning, and Feature Parsing

Like all good science experiments, we will start off with a hypothesis. In this case, we assume that papers published at about the same time and in similar fields of study will be the most useful to users. We will take a naive approach of parsing out these fields from a subsample of the overall dataset. After generating simple sparse arrays, we'll run the entire item array through an item-based collaborative filter to see if we get good results.

The item-based collaborative filter depends on a similarity score to compare items. In this case, the cosine similarity provides a reasonable comparison between two non-zero vectors. The following example actually uses the cosine distance, which is the complement of the cosine similarity in the positive space, or:

$$D_C(A,B) = 1 - S_C(A,B)$$

where D_C is the cosine distance and S_C is the cosine similarity.

Academic Paper Recommender: Naive Approach

The first step in our journey is to import and examine the dataset. In Example 9-1, we scope our experiment by limiting the fields available after the initial import. These fields are still rich in possibility, as shown in Figure 9-1.

Example 9-1. Import + filter data

```
>>> import pandas as pd

>>> model_df = pd.read_json('data/mag_papers_0/mag_subset20K.txt', lines=True)
>>> model_df.shape
(20000, 19)
>>> model_df.columns
Index(['abstract', 'authors', 'doc_type', 'doi', 'fos', 'id', 'issue',
       'keywords', 'lang', 'n_citation', 'page_end', 'page_start', 'publisher',
       'references', 'title', 'url', 'venue', 'volume', 'year'],
      dtype='object')

# filter out non-English articles and focus on a few variables
>>> model_df = model_df[model_df.lang == 'en']
...            .drop_duplicates(subset='title', keep='first')
...            .drop(['doc_type', 'doi', 'id', 'issue', 'lang', 'n_citation',
...                   'page_end', 'page_start', 'publisher', 'references',
...                   'url', 'venue', 'volume'],
...                 axis=1)
>>> model_df.shape
(10399, 6)
```

	abstract	authors	fos	keywords	title	year
0	A system and method for maskless direct write ...	NaN	[Electronic engineering, Computer hardware, En...	NaN	System and Method for Maskless Direct Write Li...	2015
1	NaN	[{'name': 'Ahmed M. Alluwaimi'}]	[Biology, Virology, Immunology, Microbiology]	[paratuberculosis, of, subspecies, proceedings...	The dilemma of the Mycobacterium avium subspec...	2016

Figure 9-1. First two rows of the Microsoft Academic Graph dataset

Table 9-1 summarizes best how further wrangling is needed to get the raw data into a better shape for a model. Lists and dictionaries are good for data storage, but are not tidy or well suited for machine learning without some unpacking (Wickham, 2014).

Table 9-1. Data schema for model_df

Field name	Description	Field type	# NaN
abstract	paper abstract	string	4393
authors	author names and affiliations	list of dict, keys = name, org	1
fos	fields of study	list of strings	1733
keywords	keywords	list of strings	4294
title	paper title	string	0
year	published year	int	0

We focus first on two fields in Example 9-2, transforming them from lists and integers into a feature array, as shown in Figure 9-2.

Example 9-2. Collaborative filtering stage 1: Build item feature matrix

```
>>> unique_fos = sorted(list({feature
...                          for paper_row in model_df.fos.fillna('0')
...                          for feature in paper_row }))

>>> unique_year = sorted(model_df['year'].astype('str').unique())
>>> def feature_array(x, var, unique_array):
...     row_dict = {}
...     for i in x.index:
...         var_dict = {}
...         for j in range(len(unique_array)):
...             if type(x[i]) is list:
...                 if unique_array[j] in x[i]:
...                     var_dict.update({var + '_' + unique_array[j]: 1})
...                 else:
...                     var_dict.update({var + '_' + unique_array[j]: 0})
...             else:
...                 if unique_array[j] == str(x[i]):
...                     var_dict.update({var + '_' + unique_array[j]: 1})
...                 else:
...                     var_dict.update({var + '_' + unique_array[j]: 0})
...         row_dict.update({i : var_dict})
...     feature_df = pd.DataFrame.from_dict(row_dict, dtype='str').T
...     return feature_df
```

```
>>> year_features = feature_array(model_df['year'], unique_year)
>>> fos_features = feature_array(model_df['fos'], unique_fos)

>>> first_features = fos_features.join(year_features).T

>>> from sys import getsizeof
>>> print('Size of first feature array: ', getsizeof(first_features))
Size of first feature array: 2583077234
```

	0	1	2	5	7	8	9	10	11	12	...	19985	19986	19987	19988	19993	19994	19995	19997	19998	19999
0	0	0	0	0	0	0	0	0	0	0	...	0	0	0	0	0	0	0	0	0	0
0-10 V lighting control	0	0	0	0	0	0	0	0	0	0	...	0	0	0	0	0	0	0	0	0	0
1/N expansion	0	0	0	0	0	0	0	0	0	0	...	0	0	0	0	0	0	0	0	0	0
10G-PON	0	0	0	0	0	0	0	0	0	0	...	0	0	0	0	0	0	0	0	0	0
14-3-3 protein	0	0	0	0	0	0	0	0	0	0	...	0	0	0	0	0	0	0	0	0	0

5 rows × 10399 columns

Figure 9-2. Head of first_features—observations' (papers') indices from the original data set are columns, features are rows

We have now successfully turned a relatively small dataset, ~10K rows of raw data, into 2.5 GB of features. But this path is too sluggish for quick, iterative exploration. We need methods that will be faster and result in features that will consume less computational resources and experimentation time.

For now, though, let's see how our current features perform at giving us a good recommendation in the next stage (Example 9-3). We'll define a "good" recommendation as a paper that looks similar to the input.

Example 9-3. Collaborative filtering stage 2: Search for similar items

```
>>> from scipy.spatial.distance import cosine

>>> def item_collab_filter(features_df):
...     item_similarities = pd.DataFrame(index = features_df.columns,
...                                      columns = features_df.columns)
...     for i in features_df.columns:
...         for j in features_df.columns:
...             item_similarities.loc[i][j] = 1 - cosine(features_df[i],
...                                                       features_df[j])
...     return item_similarities

>>> first_items = item_collab_filter(first_features.loc[:, 0:1000])
```

Why does it take so long for us to calculate the item similarities using only two features? We are taking the dot product of a 10,399 × 1,000 matrix using a nested for loop. The time per loop increases as we increase the number of observations we add to the model. Remember, this is a subset of the total available dataset, filtered for English-only papers. As we move closer to a "good" result, we'll need to go back and test on the larger set for our best results.

How can we make this faster? Since we only need one result at a time, we can change our function so that we only calculate one item at a time, specifying the number of top results we want. We'll do this later, as we continue to move through our experiment. For now, it is useful to see the full feature space to get an understanding of the impact of iterative work on brute-forcing our way through a real-world dataset.

We need to get a better idea of how these features will translate to us getting a good recommendation. Do we have enough observations to move forward? Let's plot a heatmap (Example 9-4) to see if we have any papers that are similar to each other. Figure 9-3 shows the result.

Example 9-4. Heatmap of paper recommendations

```
>>> import matplotlib.pyplot as plt
>>> import seaborn as sns
>>> import numpy as np
>>> %matplotlib inline
>>> sns.set()
>>> ax = sns.heatmap(first_items.fillna(0),
...                   vmin=0, vmax=1,
...                   cmap="YlGnBu",
...                   xticklabels=250, yticklabels=250)
>>> ax.tick_params(labelsize=12)
```

Darker pixels signal items that are similar to one another. The dark diagonal line shows that the cosine similarity is correctly indicating that each paper is most similar to itself. However, because there are a lot of NaNs for one of our features, the line is broken along the diagonal. We can see that while most of the items are not similar to one another—i.e., our dataset is fairly diverse—there are some other high-scoring candidates. These may or may not be good recommendations qualitatively, but at least we can see that our methods are not so mad.

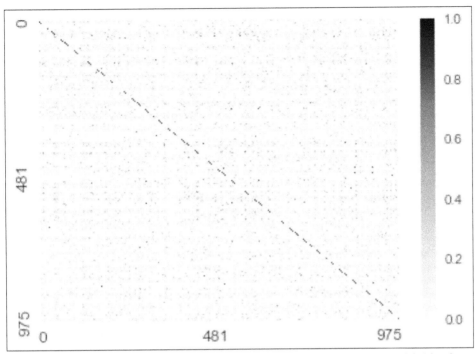

Figure 9-3. Heatmap of similar papers based on two raw features: year and fields of study

Example 9-5 shows how to translate these item similarities into a recommendation. The good news is that we have a wide variety of features still available, with lots of room for improvement.

Example 9-5. Item-based collaborative filtering recommendations

```
>>> def paper_recommender(paper_ix, items_df):
...     print('Based on the paper: \nindex = ', paper_ix)
...     print(model_df.iloc[paper_ix])
...     top_results = items_df.loc[paper_ix].sort_values(ascending=False).head(4)
...     print('\nTop three results: ')
...     order = 1
...     for i in top_results.index.tolist()[-3:]:
...         print(order,'. Paper index = ', i)
...         print('Similarity score: ', top_results[i])
...         print(model_df.iloc[i], '\n')
...         if order < 5: order += 1

>>> paper_recommender(2, first_items)

Based on the paper:
index = 2
```

```
abstract                                                 NaN
authors         [{'name': 'Jovana P. Lekovich', 'org': 'Weill ...
fos                                                      NaN
keywords                                                 NaN
title           Should endometriosis be an indication for intr...
year                                                    2015
Name: 2, dtype: object

Top three results:
1 . Paper index =  2
Similarity score:  1.0
abstract                                                 NaN
authors         [{'name': 'Jovana P. Lekovich', 'org': 'Weill ...
fos                                                      NaN
keywords                                                 NaN
title           Should endometriosis be an indication for intr...
year                                                    2015
Name: 2, dtype: object

2 . Paper index =  292
Similarity score:  1.0
abstract                                                 NaN
authors         [{'name': 'John C. Newton'}, {'name': 'Beers M...
fos             [Wide area multilateration, Maneuvering speed,...
keywords                                                 NaN
title                         Automatic speed control for aircraft
year                                                    1955
Name: 561, dtype: object

3 . Paper index =  593
Similarity score:  1.0
abstract        This paper demonstrates that on-site greywater...
authors         [{'name': 'Eran Friedler', 'org': 'Division of...
fos             [Public opinion, Environmental Engineering, Wa...
keywords        [economic analysis, tratamiento desperdicios, ...
title           The water saving potential and the socio-econo...
year                                                    2008
Name: 1152, dtype: object
```

Yikes. The good news is that the most similar paper returned is the one we are looking for. The bad news is that the next two papers don't seem to be very close to our initial search, even for the features we have chosen.

"Yes, yes," you may say, "but this is the era of Big Data! That will solve our problems! Can't we just push more data through for better results?" Potentially. But even Big Data cannot compensate for poor data and engineering choices.

Figure 9-4. Machine learning (https://xkcd.com/1838/)

Our current brute-force methods are too slow for smart, iterative engineering. Let's try some of our new feature engineering tricks to see if we can speed up the computation time and find better features and a better way to search for results.

Second Pass: More Engineering and a Smarter Model

The initial approach of creating a large, sparse array and shoving it through a filter can be improved in many ways. The next steps will focus specifically on applying better techniques to the two initial features and altering the item-based collaborative filter method for faster iteration.

First, it is time to try out some of those great feature engineering tricks for the two variables in our hypothesis. Looking deeper into the features already developed, we can choose techniques that will address each type of variable and convert it to a "better" feature for our recommendation system.

Academic Paper Recommender: Take 2

Let's focus on the *year* first. In "Quantization or Binning" on page 10, we reviewed how using raw counts for features can be problematic for methods using similarity metrics. Example 9-6 (and Figure 9-5) will examine how we can transform `'year'` to better fit the model we have selected.

Example 9-6. Fixed-width binning + dummy coding (part 1)

```
>>> print("Year spread: ", model_df['year'].min()," - ", model_df['year'].max())
>>> print("Quantile spread:\n", model_df['year'].quantile([0.25, 0.5, 0.75]))
Year spread:  1831  -  2017
Quantile spread:
0.25    1990.0
0.50    2005.0
0.75    2012.0
Name: year, dtype: float64

# plot years to see the distribution
>>> fig, ax = plt.subplots()
>>> model_df['year'].hist(ax=ax,
...                       bins= model_df['year'].max() - model_df['year'].min())
>>> ax.tick_params(labelsize=12)
>>> ax.set_xlabel('Year Count', fontsize=12)
>>> ax.set_ylabel('Occurrence', fontsize=12)
```

We can see from the skewed distribution (Figure 9-5) that this is an excellent candidate for binning.

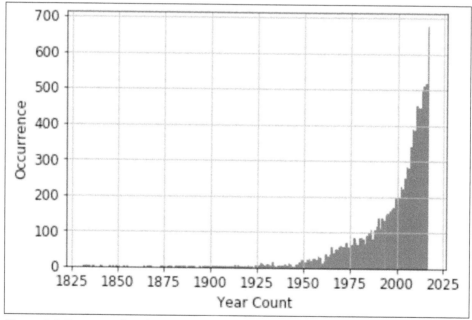

Figure 9-5. Raw year distribution for 10K+ academic papers in dataset

The bins will be based on ranges within the variable, rather than the unique number of features. To further reduce the feature space, we will dummy-code the resultant bins (see Example 9-7). Pandas can do both using built-in functions. These methods will make our results easy to interpret, so we can do a quick check of the transformed features before moving on (see Figure 9-6).

Example 9-7. Fixed-width binning + dummy coding (part 2)

```
# binning here (by 10 years) reduces the year feature space from 156 to 19
>>> bins = int(round((model_df['year'].max() - model_df['year'].min()) / 10))

>>> temp_df = pd.DataFrame(index = model_df.index)
>>> temp_df['yearBinned'] = pd.cut(model_df['year'].tolist(), bins, precision = 0)
>>> X_yrs = pd.get_dummies(temp_df['yearBinned'])
>>> X_yrs.columns.categories
IntervalIndex([[(1831.0, 1841.0], (1841.0, 1851.0], (1851.0, 1860.0],
                (1860.0, 1870.0], (1870.0, 1880.0] ... (1968.0, 1978.0],
                (1978.0, 1988.0], (1988.0, 1997.0], (1997.0, 2007.0],
                (2007.0, 2017.0]]
               closed='right',
               dtype='interval[float64]')

# plot the new distribution
>>> fig, ax = plt.subplots()
>>> X_yrs.sum().plot.bar(ax = ax)
>>> ax.tick_params(labelsize=8)
>>> ax.set_xlabel('Binned Years', fontsize=12)
>>> ax.set_ylabel('Counts', fontsize=12)
```

We have preserved the underlying distribution of the original variable through binning by decades. If we desired to use a method that would benefit from a different distribution, we could alter our binning choices to change how this variable presents itself to the model. Since we are using cosine similarity, this is fine. Let's move on to the next feature we originally included in our model.

The fields-of-study feature space contributed significantly to the original model's size and processing time.

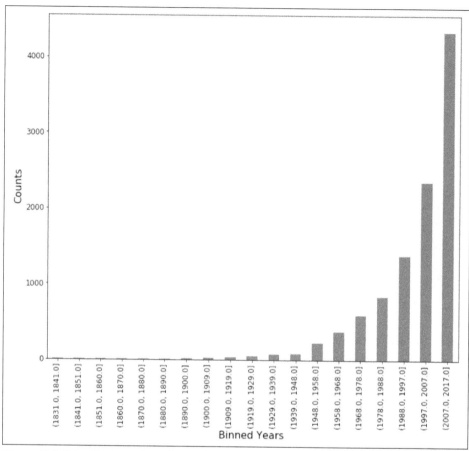

Figure 9-6. Distribution of new binned X_yrs feature

Let's examine the work we have already done. By parsing out the list of strings, we created a "bag-of-phrases" in the first pass. Since we already have a useful sparse array, we can focus on using a more efficient data type. Example 9-8 illustrates how converting from a Pandas DataFrame to a NumPy sparse array affects computation time.

Example 9-8. Converting bag-of-phrases pd.Series to NumPy sparse array

```
>>> X_fos = fos_features.values

# We can see how this will make a difference in the future by looking
# at the size of each
>>> print('Our pandas Series, in bytes: ', getsizeof(fos_features))
>>> print('Our hashed numpy array, in bytes: ', getsizeof(X_fos))
```

```
Our pandas Series, in bytes:  2530632380
Our hashed numpy array, in bytes:  112
```

Much better! Putting it back together, we'll pipe our features together (Example 9-9) and rerun our recommender (Example 9-10) to see if we have improved results, taking advantage of scikit-learn's cosine similarity function. We will also reduce the computational time by only focusing on one item at a time.

Example 9-9. Collaborative filtering stages 1 + 2: Build item feature matrix, search for similar items

```
>>> second_features = np.append(X_fos, X_yrs, axis = 1)
>>> print("The power of feature engineering saves us, in bytes: ",
...        getsizeof(first_features) - getsizeof(second_features))
The power of feature engineering saves us, in bytes:  168066769

>>> from sklearn.metrics.pairwise import cosine_similarity

>>> def piped_collab_filter(features_matrix, index, top_n):
...     item_similarities = \
...         1 - cosine_similarity(features_matrix[index:index+1],
...                               features_matrix).flatten()
...     related_indices = \
...         [i for i in item_similarities.argsort()[::-1] if i != index]
...     return [(index, item_similarities[index])
...             for index in related_indices
...             ][0:top_n]
```

Example 9-10. Item-based collaborative filtering recommendations: Take 2

```
>>> def paper_recommender(items_df, paper_ix, top_n):
...     if paper_ix in model_df.index:
...         print('Based on the paper:')
...         print('Paper index = ', model_df.loc[paper_ix].name)
...         print('Title :', model_df.loc[paper_ix]['title'])
...         print('FOS :', model_df.loc[paper_ix]['fos'])
...         print('Year :', model_df.loc[paper_ix]['year'])
...         print('Abstract :', model_df.loc[paper_ix]['abstract'])
...         print('Authors :', model_df.loc[paper_ix]['authors'], '\n')
...         # define the location index for the DataFrame index requested
...         array_ix = model_df.index.get_loc(paper_ix)
...         top_results = piped_collab_filter(items_df, array_ix, top_n)
...         print('\nTop',top_n,'results: ')

...         order = 1
...         for i in range(len(top_results)):
...             print(order,'. Paper index = ',
...                 model_df.iloc[top_results[i][0]].name)
...             print('Similarity score: ', top_results[i][1])
...             print('Title :', model_df.iloc[top_results[i][0]]['title'])
```

```
...              print('FOS :', model_df.iloc[top_results[i][0]]['fos'])
...              print('Year :', model_df.iloc[top_results[i][0]]['year'])
...              print('Abstract :', model_df.iloc[top_results[i][0]]['abstract'])
...              print('Authors :', model_df.iloc[top_results[i][0]]['authors'],
...                   '\n')
...              if order < top_n: order += 1
...      else:
...          print('Whoops! Choose another paper. Try something from here: \n',
...                model_df.index[100:200])

>>> paper_recommender(second_features, 2, 3)
Based on the paper:
Paper index = 2
Title : Should endometriosis be an indication for intracytoplasmic sperm inject ...
FOS : nan
Year : 2015
Abstract : nan
Authors : [{'name': 'Jovana P. Lekovich', 'org': 'Weill Cornell Medical College, ...

Top 3 results:
1 . Paper index = 10055
Similarity score: 1.0
Title : [Diagnosis of cerebral tumors; comparative studies on arteriography, ...
FOS : ['Radiology', 'Pathology', 'Surgery']
Year : 1953
Abstract : nan
Authors : [{'name': 'Antoine'}, {'name': 'Lepoire'}, {'name': 'Schoumacker'}]

2 . Paper index = 11771
Similarity score: 1.0
Title : A Study of Special Functions in the Theory of Eclipsing Binary Systems
FOS : ['Contact binary']
Year : 1981
Abstract : nan
Authors : [{'name': 'Filaretti Zafiropoulos', 'org': 'University of Manchester'}]

3 . Paper index = 11773
Similarity score: 1.0
Title : Studies of powder flow using a recording powder flowmeter and measure ...
FOS : nan
Year : 1985
Abstract : This paper describes the utility of the dynamic measurement of the ...
Authors : [{'name': 'Ramachandra P. Hegde', 'org': 'Department of Pharmacy, ...
```

To be honest, I don't think our feature selection is working out too well. There is a lot of missing data in these fields. Let's keep going to see if we can choose richer features with more information.

Finding Your Place

Converting between Pandas DataFrames and NumPy matrices can make indices tricky—we have the same size index, but the index assignments are not the same. Pandas assists with this using .iloc, .loc, and .get_loc, as we show in Example 9-11:

- .loc returns the index based on the original Pandas DataFrame, allowing us to reference specific papers.
- .iloc uses the integer location, which is the same index as our NumPy array.
- .get_loc helps us find the integer location when we know the DataFrame index.

Example 9-11. Maintaining index assignment during conversions

```
>>> model_df.loc[21]
abstract     A microprocessor includes hardware registers t...
authors                       [{'name': 'Mark John Ebersole'}]
fos          [Embedded system, Parallel computing, Computer...
keywords                                                   NaN
title        Microprocessor that enables ARM ISA program to...
year                                                      2013
Name: 21, dtype: object

>>> model_df.iloc[21]
abstract                                                   NaN
authors      [{'name': 'Nicola M. Heller'}, {'name': 'Steph...
fos          [Biology, Medicine, Post-transcriptional regul...
keywords     [glucocorticoids, post transcriptional regulat...
title        Post-transcriptional regulation of eotaxin by ...
year                                                      2002
Name: 30, dtype: object

>>> model_df.index.get_loc(30)
21
```

Third Pass: More Features = More Information

Our experiment thus far is not supporting the original hypothesis that *year* and *fields-of-study* would be sufficient to recommend a similar paper. At this point, we have a few options:

- Upload more of the original dataset to see if we get better results.
- Spend more time exploring the data to examine if we have a sufficiently dense set to provide good recommendations.
- Iterate on the current model by adding more features.

The first option makes the assumption that the problem is in our sampling of the data. This might be the case, but is similar to Figure 9-4's analogy of stirring the data pile for better results.

The second option would give a better idea of the underlying raw data. This should be continually revisited based on how your decisions for features and model selection change during the exploration process. The initial subsample chosen here reflects this step. Since we have more variables available in the dataset, we will not go back here yet.

This leaves the third option, moving forward on our current model by adding more features. Providing more information about each item can improve the similarity scores and result in better recommendations.

Based on our initial exploration, the next steps will focus on the fields with the most information, *abstract* and *authors*.

Academic Paper Recommender: Take 3

Looking back at Chapter 4, we can see that *abstract* is a good candidate for tf-idf to filter through the noise and find the salient associative words. We do this in Example 9-12.

Example 9-12. Stopwords + tf-idf

```
# need to fill in NaN for sklearn use in future
>>> filled_df = model_df.fillna('None')

>>> from sklearn.feature_extraction.text import TfidfVectorizer

>>> vectorizer = TfidfVectorizer(sublinear_tf=True, max_df=0.5,
...                              stop_words='english')
>>> X_abstract = vectorizer.fit_transform(filled_df['abstract'])
>>> third_features = np.append(second_features, X_abstract.toarray(), axis = 1)
```

We can reduce the computational load of the messy and uneven *authors* by wrangling into a dictionary and then running it through a one-hot encoder, as shown in Example 9-13.

Example 9-13. One-hot encoding using scikit-learn's DictVectorizer

```
>>> authors_list = []

>>> for row in filled_df.authors.itertuples():
...     # create a dictionary from each Series index
...     if type(row.authors) is str:
...         y = {'None': row.Index}
...     if type(row.authors) is list:
```

```
...             # add these keys + values to our running dictionary
...             y = dict.fromkeys(row.authors[0].values(), row.Index)
...          authors_list.append(y)

>>> authors_list[0:5]
[{'None': 0},
 {'Ahmed M. Alluwaimi': 1},
 {'Jovana P. Lekovich': 2, 'Weill Cornell Medical College, New York, NY': 2},
 {'George C. Sponsler': 5},
 {'M. T. Richards': 7}]

>>> from sklearn.feature_extraction import DictVectorizer
>>> v = DictVectorizer(sparse=False)
>>> D = authors_list
>>> X_authors = v.fit_transform(D)
>>> fourth_features = np.append(third_features, X_authors, axis = 1)
```

Time to check in with the recommender to see how these new features are working out. Example 9-14 shows the results.

Example 9-14. Item-based collaborative filtering recommendations: Take 3

```
>>> paper_recommender(fourth_features, 2, 3)

Based on the paper:
Paper index =  2
Title : Should endometriosis be an indication for intracytoplasmic sperm inject ...
FOS : nan
Year : 2015
Abstract : nan
Authors : [{'name': 'Jovana P. Lekovich', 'org': 'Weill Cornell Medical College, ...


Top 3 results:
1 . Paper index =  10055
Similarity score:  1.0
Title : [Diagnosis of cerebral tumors; comparative studies on arteriography, ...
FOS : ['Radiology', 'Pathology', 'Surgery']
Year : 1953
Abstract : nan
Authors : [{'name': 'Antoine'}, {'name': 'Lepoire'}, {'name': 'Schoumacker'}]

2 . Paper index =  5601
Similarity score:  1.0
Title : 633 Survival after coronary revascularization, with and without mitral ...
FOS : ['Cardiology']
Year : 2005
Abstract : nan
Authors : [{'name': 'J.B. Le Polain De Waroux'}, {'name': 'Anne-Catherine ...

3 . Paper index =  12256
```

```
Similarity score:  1.0
Title : Nucleotide Sequence and Analysis of an Insertion Sequence from Bacillus ...
FOS : ['Biology', 'Molecular biology', 'Insertion sequence', 'Nucleic acid ...
Year : 1994
Abstract : A 5.8-kb DNA fragment encoding the  cryIC  gene from  Bacillus thur...
Authors : [{'name': 'Geoffrey P. Smith'}, {'name': 'David J. Ellar'}, {'name': ...
```

Even accounting for missing data in certain fields, the top three results from the last round of feature engineering are directing us to other papers in the medical field.

The range of papers represented in this dataset is broad; for example, a random sample of papers exposed fields of study such as "Coupling constant," "Evapotranspiration," "Hash function," "IVMS," "Meditation," "Pareto analysis," "Second-generation wavelet transform," "Slip," and "Spiral galaxy." Given that there are 7,604 unique fields of study listed for 10K+ papers, these last results seem to be moving in the right direction. We can be confident that our work is progressing toward a useful model.

Continued iteration on more text variables, such as the finding the noun phrases of the paper titles or stemming the keywords, could bring us even closer to a "best" recommendation.

It should be noted here that this definition of "best" is the Holy Grail of all recommenders and search engines alike. We are searching for what a user will find most helpful, which may or may not be directly represented by the data. Feature engineering allows us to abstract salient features into representations such that algorithms can expose both the explicit and implicit information contained therein.

Summary

As you can see, building models for machine learning is easy. Building *good* models for *useful* results takes time and work. We hiked through the messy processes here of examining a collection of possible variables and experimenting with different feature engineering methods to achieve better results. We define "better" here not just in terms of good outcomes from our training and testing, but also reducing the size of the model and the time it takes us to iterate over different experiments.

We started this book by talking about how mastery of a subject comes from deeply learning the principles at work, in order to gain intuition to effectively put your knowledge to work. We hope that our work has given you the necessary tools to become more efficient and effective, as well as enriched your mathematical and computational understanding of how feature engineering is an essential skill to develop useful machine learning models.

Bibliography

Sarwar, Badrul, George Karypis, Joseph Konstan, and John Riedl. "Item-Based Collaborative Filtering Recommendation Algorithms." *Proceedings of the 10th International Conference on the World Wide Web* (2001) 285–295.

Sinha, Arnab, Zhihong Shen, Yang Song, Hao Ma, Darrin Eide, Bo-June (Paul) Hsu, and Kuansan Wang. "An Overview of Microsoft Academic Service (MAS) and Applications." *Proceedings of the 24th International Conference on the World Wide Web* (2015): 243–246.

Tang, Jie, Jing Zhang, Limin Yao, Juanzi Li, Li Zhang, and Zhong Su. "ArnetMiner: Extraction and Mining of Academic Social Networks." *Proceedings of the 14th ACM SIGKDD International Conference on Knowledge Discovery and Data Mining* (2008): 990–998.

Wickham, Hadley. "Tidy Data." *The Journal of Statistical Software* 59 (2014).

Linear Modeling and Linear Algebra Basics

Overview of Linear Classification

When we have a labeled dataset, the feature space is strewn with data points from different classes. It is the job of the classifier to separate the data points from different classes. It can do so by producing an output that is very different for data points from one class versus another. For instance, when there are only two classes, then a good classifier should produce large outputs for one class, and small ones for another. The points right on the cusp of being in one class versus another form a *decision surface* (Figure A-1).

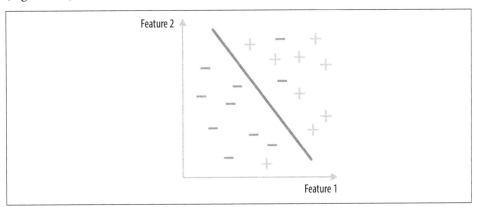

Figure A-1. Simple binary classification finds a surface that separates two classes of data points

Many functions can be made into classifiers. It's a good idea to look for the *simplest* function that cleanly separates the classes, for a few reasons. First of all, it's easier to find the best simple separator than the best complex separator. Also, simple functions often generalize better to new data, because it's harder to tailor them too specifically to the training data (a concept known as *overfitting*). A simple model might make mistakes—like in Figure A-1, where some points are on the wrong side of the divide—but we're willing to sacrifice some training accuracy in order to have a simpler decision surface that can achieve better test accuracy. The principle of minimizing complexity and maximizing usefulness is called "Occam's razor," and is widely applicable in science and engineering.

The simplest function is a line. A *linear function* of one input variable is a familiar sight (Figure A-2).

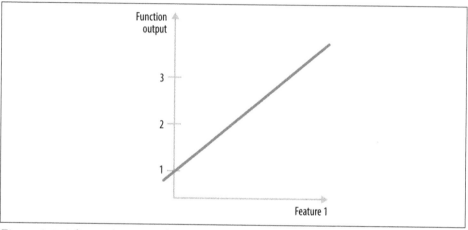

Figure A-2. A linear function of one input variable

A linear function with two input variables can be visualized as either a flat plane in 3D or a contour plot in 2D (shown in Figure A-3). Like a topological geographic map, each line of the contour plot represents points in the input space that have the same output.

It's harder to visualize higher-dimensional linear functions, which are called *hyperplanes*. But it's easy enough to write down the algebraic formula. A multidimensional linear function has a set of inputs $x_1, x_2, ..., x_n$ and a set of weight parameters $w_0, w_1, ..., w_n$:

$$f_w(x_1, x_2, ..., x_n) = w_0 + w_1 {}^* x_1 + w_2 {}^* x_2 + ... + w_n {}^* x_n$$

It can be written more succinctly using vector notation:

$$f_w(\mathbf{x}) = \mathbf{x}^T \mathbf{w}$$

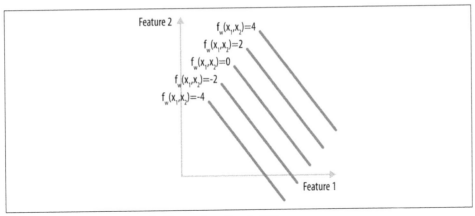

Figure A-3. Contour plot of a linear function in 2D

We follow the usual convention for mathematical notations, which uses boldface to indicate a vector and non-boldface to indicate a scalar. The vector **x** is padded with an extra 1 at the beginning, as a placeholder for the intercept term w_0. If all input features are 0, then the output of the function is w_0. So, w_0 is also known as the *bias* or *intercept term*.

Training a linear classifier is equivalent to picking out the best separating hyperplane between the classes. This translates into finding the best vector **w** that is oriented exactly right in space. Since each data point has a target label y, we could find a **w** that tries to directly emulate the target label:[1]

$$\mathbf{x}^T\mathbf{w} = \mathbf{y}$$

Since there is usually more than one data point, we want a **w** that simultaneously makes all of the predictions close to the target labels:

$$A\mathbf{w} = \mathbf{y}$$

Here, A is known as the *data matrix* (also known as the design matrix in statistics). It contains the data in a particular form: each row is a data point and each column a

---

1 Strictly speaking, the formula given here is for linear regression, not linear classification. The difference is that regression allows for real-valued target variables, whereas classification targets are usually integers that represent different classes. A regressor can be turned into a classifier via a nonlinear transform. For instance, the logistic regression classifier passes the linear transform of the input through a logistic function. Such models are called *generalized linear models* and have linear functions at their core. Even though this example is about classification, we use the formula for linear regression as a teaching tool, because it is much easier to analyze. The intuitions readily map to generalized linear classifiers.

feature. (Sometimes people also look at its transpose, where features are the rows and data points the columns.)

The Anatomy of a Matrix

In order to solve the preceding equation, we need some basic knowledge of linear algebra. For a systematic introduction to the subject, we highly recommend Strang (2006).

The equation states that when a certain matrix multiplies a certain vector, there is a certain outcome. A matrix is also called a linear operator, a name that makes it more apparent that a matrix is a little machine. This machine takes a vector as input and spits out another vector using a combination of several key operations: rotating a vector's direction, adding or subtracting dimensions, and stretching or compressing its length. This combination can be quite powerful for manipulating shapes in the input space.

For example, as Figure A-4 shows, a 3 × 2 matrix can transform a square area in 2D into a diamond-shaped area in 3D. It does so by rotating and stretching each vector in the input space into a new vector in the output space.

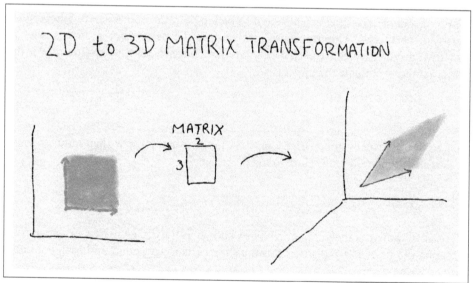

Figure A-4. A 2D to 3D matrix transformation

From Vectors to Subspaces

In order to understand a linear operator, we have to look at how it morphs the input into output. Luckily, we don't have to analyze one input vector at a time. Vectors can be organized into subspaces, and *linear operators manipulate vector subspaces.*

A subspace is a set of vectors that satisfies two criteria. First, if it contains a vector, then it contains the line that passes through the origin and that point. Second, if it contains two points, then it contains all the linear combinations of those two vectors. Linear combination is a combination of two types of operations: multiplying a vector with a scalar, and adding two vectors together.

One important property of a subspace is its *rank* or dimensionality, which is a measure of the degrees of freedom in this space. A line has rank 1, a 2D plane has rank 2, and so on. If you can imagine a multidimensional bird in our multidimensional space, then the rank of the subspace tells us in how many "independent" directions the bird could fly. "Independence" here means "linear independence": two vectors are linearly independent if one isn't a constant multiple of another (i.e., they are not pointing in exactly the same or opposite directions).

A subspace can be defined as the span of a set of *basis vectors*. (Span is a technical term that describes the set of all linear combinations of a set of vectors.) The span of a set of vectors is invariant under linear combinations (because it's defined that way). So, if we have one set of basis vectors, then we can multiply the vectors by any non-zero constants or add the vectors to get another basis.

It would be nice to have a more unique and identifiable basis to describe a subspace. An *orthonormal basis* contains vectors that have unit length and are orthogonal to each other. Orthogonality is another technical term. (At least 50% of all math and science is made up of technical terms. If you don't believe me, do a bag-of-words count on this book.) Two vectors are *orthogonal* to each other if their inner product is zero. For all intents and purposes, we can think of orthogonal vectors as being at 90 degrees to each other. (This is true in Euclidean space, which closely resembles our physical 3D reality.) Normalizing these vectors to have unit length turns them into a uniform set of measuring sticks.

All in all, a subspace is like a tent, and the orthogonal basis vectors are the number of poles at right angles that are required to prop up the tent. The rank is equal to the total number of orthogonal basis vectors. Figure A-5 illustrates some these concepts.

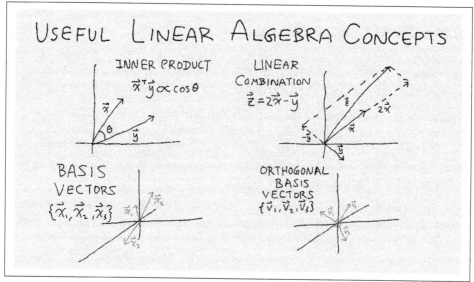

Figure A-5. Illustrations of four useful linear algebra concepts: inner product, linear combination, basis vectors, and orthogonal basis vectors

Useful Linear Algebra Definitions

For those who think in math, here is some math to make our descriptions precise:

Scalar
 A number c, in contrast to a vector.

Vector
 $\mathbf{x} = (x_1, x_2, ..., x_n)$

Linear combination
 $a\mathbf{x} + b\mathbf{y} = (ax_1 + by_1, ax_2 + by_2, ..., ax_n + by_n)$

Span of a set of vectors $\mathbf{v}_1, ..., \mathbf{v}_k$
 The set of vectors $\mathbf{u} = a_1\mathbf{v}_1 + ... + a_k\mathbf{v}_k$ for any $a_1, ..., a_k$.

Linear independence
 $\mathbf{x}$ and $\mathbf{y}$ are independent if $\mathbf{x} \neq c\mathbf{y}$ for any scalar constant c.

Inner product:
 $\langle \mathbf{x}, \mathbf{y} \rangle = x_1y_1 + x_2y_2 + ... + x_ny_n$

Orthogonal vectors
 Two vectors $\mathbf{x}$ and $\mathbf{y}$ are orthogonal if $\langle \mathbf{x}, \mathbf{y} \rangle = 0$.

Subspace
> A subset of vectors within a larger containing vector space, satisfying these three criteria:
>
> 1. It contains the zero vector.
> 2. If it contains a vector **v**, then it contains all vectors $c\mathbf{v}$, where c is a scalar.
> 3. If it contains two vectors **u** and **v**, then it contains the vector $\mathbf{u} + \mathbf{v}$.

Basis
> A set of vectors that span a subspace.

Orthogonal basis
> A basis $\{\mathbf{v}_1, \mathbf{v}_2, ..., \mathbf{v}_d\}$ where $\langle \mathbf{v}_i, \mathbf{v}_j \rangle = 0$ for all i, j.

Rank of subspace
> The minimum number of linearly independent basis vectors that span the subspace.

Singular Value Decomposition (SVD)

A matrix performs a linear transformation on the input vector. Linear transformations are very simple and constrained. It follows that a matrix can't manipulate a subspace willy-nilly. One of the most fascinating theorems of linear algebra proves that every square matrix, no matter what numbers it contains, must map a certain set of vectors back to themselves with some scaling. In the general case of a rectangular matrix, it maps a set of input vectors into a corresponding set of output vectors, and its *transpose* maps those outputs back to the original inputs. The technical terminology is that square matrices have eigenvectors with eigenvalues, and rectangular matrices have left and right singular vectors with singular values.

Eigenvector and Singular Vector

Let A be an $n \times n$ matrix. If there is a vector **v** and a scalar λ such that $A\mathbf{v} = \lambda\mathbf{v}$, then **v** is an *eigenvector* and λ an *eigenvalue* of A.

Let A be a rectangular matrix. If there are vectors **u** and **v** and a scalar σ such that $A\mathbf{v} = \sigma\mathbf{u}$ and $A^T\mathbf{u} = \sigma\mathbf{v}$, then **u** and **v** are called *left and right singular vectors* and σ is a *singular value* of A.

Algebraically, the SVD of a matrix looks like this:

$$A = U\Sigma V^T$$

where the columns of the matrices **U** and **V** form orthonormal bases of the input and output space, respectively. **Σ** is a diagonal matrix containing the singular values.

Geometrically, a matrix performs the following sequence of transformations:

1. Map the input vector onto the right singular basis vector.
2. Scale each coordinate by the corresponding singular values.
3. Multiply this score with each of the left singular vectors.
4. Sum up the results.

Figure A-6 provides an illustration. The operations go from right to left for a matrix-vector multiplication. The rightmost machine rotates and potentially projects the input into a lower-dimensional space. In this illustration, the input cube becomes a flat square, and is also rotated. The next machine squeezes the square in one direction and stretches it in another; the square becomes a rectangle. The last, leftmost machine rotates the rectangle again, and projects it back out into a possibly higher-dimensional space—but it remains a flat rectangle instead of some higher-dimensional object.

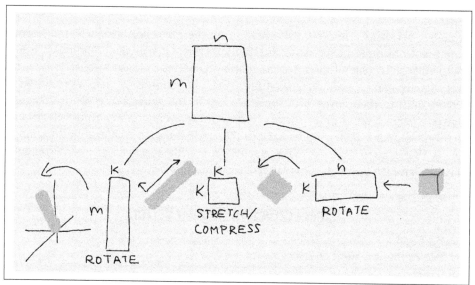

Figure A-6. A matrix decomposed into three little machines: rotate, scale, rotate

When **A** is a real matrix (i.e., all of the elements are real-valued), all of the singular values and singular vectors are real-valued. A singular value can be positive, negative, or zero. The ordered set of singular values of a matrix is called its *spectrum*, and it reveals a lot about the matrix. The gap between the singular values affects how stable the solutions are, and the ratio between the maximum and minimum absolute singular values (the *condition number*) affects how quickly an iterative solver can find the solution. Both of these properties have notable impacts on the quality of the solution one can find.

The Four Fundamental Subspaces of the Data Matrix

Another useful way to dissect a matrix is via the four fundamental subspaces: column space, row space, null space, and left null space. These four subspaces completely characterize the solutions to linear systems involving A or A^T (hence the moniker).

For the data matrix (where the rows are data points and columns are features), the four fundamental subspaces can be understood in relation to the data and features. Let's look at them in more detail.

Column space

Mathematical definition:
   The set of output vectors **s** where **s** = A**w** as we vary the weight vector **w**.

Mathematical interpretation:
   All possible linear combinations of columns.

Data interpretation:
   All outcomes that are linearly predictable based on observed features. The vector **w** contains the weight of each feature.

Basis:
   The left singular vectors corresponding to nonzero singular values (a subset of the columns of U).

Row space

Mathematical definition:
   The set of output vectors **r** where **r** = **u**$^\mathrm{T}A$ as we vary the weight vector **u**.

Mathematical interpretation:
   All possible linear combinations of rows.

Data interpretation:
   A vector in the row space is something that can be represented as a linear combination of existing data points. Hence, this can be interpreted as the space of "non-novel" data. The vector **u** contains the weight of each data point in the linear combination.

Basis:
   The right singular vectors corresponding to nonzero singular values (a subset of the columns of V).

Null space

Mathematical definition:

The set of input vectors $\mathbf{w}$ where $A\mathbf{w} = 0$.

Mathematical interpretation:

Vectors that are orthogonal to all rows of A. The null space gets squashed to zero by the matrix. This is the "fluff" that adds volume to the solution space of $A\mathbf{w} = \mathbf{y}$.

Data interpretation:

"Novel" data points that cannot be represented as any linear combination of existing data points.

Basis:

The right singular vectors corresponding to the zero singular values (the rest of the columns of V).

Left null space

Mathematical definition:

The set of input vectors $\mathbf{u}$ where $\mathbf{u}^T A = 0$.

Mathematical interpretation:

Vectors that are orthogonal to all columns of A. The left null space is orthogonal to the column space.

Data interpretation:

"Novel feature vectors" that are not representable by linear combinations of existing features.

Basis:

The left singular vectors corresponding to the zero singular values (the rest of the columns of U).

Column space and row space contain what is already representable based on observed data and features. Those vectors that lie in the column space are non-novel features. Those vectors that lie in the row space are non-novel data points.

For the purposes of modeling and prediction, non-novelty is good. A full column space means that the feature set contains enough information to model any target vector we wish. A full row space means that the different data points contain enough variation to cover all possible corners of the feature space. It's the novel data points and features—respectively contained in the null space and the left null space—that we have to worry about.

In the application of building linear models of data, the null space can also be viewed as the subspace of "novel" data points. Novelty is not a good thing in this context.

Novel data points indicate phantom data that is not linearly representable by the training set. Similarly, the left null space contains novel features that are not representable as linear combinations of existing features.

The null space is orthogonal to the row space. It's easy to see why. The definition of null space states that $\mathbf{w}$ has an inner product of 0 with every row vector in A. Therefore, $\mathbf{w}$ is orthogonal to the space spanned by these row vectors, i.e., the row space. Similarly, the left null space is orthogonal to the column space.

Solving a Linear System

Let's tie all this math back to the problem at hand: training a linear classifier, which is intimately connected to the task of solving a linear system. We look closely at how a matrix operates because we have to reverse engineer it. In order to train a linear model, we have to find the input weight vector $\mathbf{w}$ that maps to the observed output targets $\mathbf{y}$ in the system $A\mathbf{w} = \mathbf{y}$, where A is the data matrix.[2]

Let's try to crank the machine of the linear operator in reverse. If we had the SVD decomposition of A, then we could map $\mathbf{y}$ onto the left singular vectors (columns of U), reverse the scaling factors (multiply by the inverse of the nonzero singular values), and finally map them back to the right singular vectors (columns of V). Ta-da! Simple, right?

This is in fact the process of computing the *pseudo-inverse* of A. It makes use of a key property of an orthonormal basis: the transpose is the inverse. This is why SVD is so powerful. (In practice, real linear system solvers do not use the SVD, because it's rather expensive to compute. There are other, much cheaper ways to decompose a matrix, such as QR (*http://bit.ly/2D51LU1*) or LU (*http://bit.ly/2Fosjl6*) or Cholesky (*http://bit.ly/2IbRlFQ*) decompositions.)

However, we skipped one tiny little detail in our haste. What happens if the singular value is zero? We can't take the inverse of 0 because $1/0 = \infty$. This is why it's called the pseudo-inverse. (The real inverse isn't even defined for rectangular matrices. Only square matrices have them, as long as all of the eigenvalues are nonzero.) A singular value of zero squashes whatever input was given; there's no way to retrace its steps and come up with the original input.

---

2 Actually, it's a little more complicated than that. y may not be in the column space of A, so there may not be a solution to this equation. Instead of giving up, statistical machine learning looks for an approximate solution. It defines a loss function that quantifies the quality of a solution. If the solution is exact, then the loss is 0. Small errors, small loss; big errors, big loss, and so on. The training process then looks for the best parameters that minimize this loss function. In ordinary linear regression, the loss function is called the squared residual loss, which essentially maps y to the closest point in the column space of A. Logistic regression minimizes the log loss. In both cases, and linear models in general, the linear system $A\mathbf{w}=\mathbf{y}$ often lies at the core. Hence, our analysis here is very much relevant.

Okay, going backward we get stuck on this one little detail. Let's take what we've got and go forward again to see if we can unjam the machine. Suppose we came up with an answer to $A\mathbf{w} = \mathbf{y}$. Let's call it $\mathbf{w}_{particular}$, because it's particularly suited for $\mathbf{y}$. Suppose that there are also a bunch of input vectors that A squashes to zero. Let's take one of them and call it $\mathbf{w}_{sad\text{-}trumpet}$, because wah wah. Then, what do you think happens when we add $\mathbf{w}_{particular}$ to $\mathbf{w}_{sad\text{-}trumpet}$?

$$A(\mathbf{w}_{particular} + \mathbf{w}_{sad\text{-}trumpet}) = \mathbf{y}$$

Amazing! So this is a solution too. In fact, any input that gets squashed to zero could be added to a particular solution and give us another solution. The general solution looks like this:

$$\mathbf{w}_{general} = \mathbf{w}_{particular} + \mathbf{w}_{homogeneous}$$

$\mathbf{w}_{particular}$ is an exact solution to the equation $A\mathbf{w} = \mathbf{y}$. There may or may not be such a solution. If there isn't, then the system can only be approximately solved. If there is, then $\mathbf{y}$ belongs to what's known as the column space of A. The column space is the set of vectors that A can map *to*, by taking linear combinations of its columns.

$\mathbf{w}_{homogeneous}$ is a solution to the equation $A\mathbf{w} = 0$. (The grown-up name for $\mathbf{w}_{sad\text{-}trumpet}$ is $\mathbf{w}_{homogeneous}$.) This should now look familiar. The set of all $\mathbf{w}_{homogeneous}$ vectors forms the null space of A. This is the span of the right singular vectors with singular value 0.

The name "null space" sounds like the destination of woe for an existential crisis. If the null space contains any vectors other than the all-zero vector, then there are infinitely many solutions to the equation $A\mathbf{w} = \mathbf{y}$. Having too many solutions to choose from is not in itself a bad thing. Sometimes any solution will do. But if there are many possible answers, then there are many sets of features that are useful for the classification task. It becomes difficult to understand which ones are truly important.

One way to fix the problem of a large null space is to *regulate* the model by adding additional constraints:

$$A\mathbf{w} = \mathbf{y},$$

where $\mathbf{w}$ is such that $\mathbf{w}^\mathsf{T}\mathbf{w} = c$.

This form of regularization constrains the weight vector to have a certain norm, c. The strength of this regularization is controlled by a regularization parameter, which must be tuned, as is done in our experiments.

In general, *feature selection* methods deal with selecting the most useful features to reduce computation burden, decrease the amount of confusion for the model, and make the learned model more unique. This is the focus of "Feature Selection" on page 38.

Another problem is the "unevenness" of the spectrum of the data matrix. When we train a linear classifier, we care not only that there is a general solution to the linear system, but also that we can find it easily. Typically, the training process employs a solver that works by calculating a gradient of the loss function and walking downhill in small steps. When some singular values are very large and others very close to zero, the solver needs to carefully step around the longer singular vectors (those that correspond to large singular values) and spend a lot of time digging around in the shorter singular vectors to find the true answer. This "unevenness" in the spectrum is measured by the condition number of the matrix, which is basically the ratio between the largest and the smallest absolute value of the singular values.

To summarize, in order for there to be a good linear model that is relatively unique, and in order for it to be easy to find, we wish for the following:

1. The label vector can be well approximated by a linear combination of a subset of features (column vectors). Better yet, the set of features should be linearly independent.
2. In order for the null space to be small, the row space must be large. (This is due to the fact that the two subspaces are orthogonal.) The more linearly independent the set of data points (row vectors), the smaller the null space.
3. In order for the solution to be easy to find, the condition number of the data matrix—the ratio between the maximum and minimum singular values—should be small.

Bibliography

Strang, Gilbert. *Linear Algebra and Its Applications*. 4th ed. Boston, MA: Cengage Learning, 2006.

Index

Symbols

ℓ^2 normalization, 32, 65, 66, 108, 117
    cross validation classifier accuracy, 72

A

academic paper recommender (see recommender for academic papers)
activation functions, 150
AlexNet, 144
    convolutional layers, 150
    fully connected layers, 145
    pooling layers, 153
    ReLU transformation, 151
    response normalization layers, 151
    structure of, 153-157
anomaly detection of time series, use of PCA, 111
approximately leakage-proof statistics, 93
ASCII, 52
audio data, 133

B

back-off bin, 91
bag-of-n-grams, 45
bag-of-words (BoW) featurization, 42
    scaling with tf-idf transformation, 65
basis vectors, 183, 185
bias, 181
"Big Learning Made Easy—With Counts!" blog post, 87
bigrams, 45
Bilenko, Misha, 87
bin counting, 78, 87-94
    counts without bounds, 94

    example of, 87
    example, using data from Avazu Kaggle competition, 90
    guarding against data leakage, 93
    odds ratio and log odds ratio for, 88
    one-hot encoding vs., 89
    rare categories, 91
    trade-offs, 95
binarization (of counts), 9
binning
    fixed-width, 12
    quantile, 13
binomial distribution, 55
Box-Cox transforms, 24

C

C-HOG blocks, 142
categorical variables, 77-97
    encodings, 78-83
        dummy coding, 79-82
        effect coding, 82
        one-hot encoding, 78
        pros and cons of, 83
    large, dealing with, 83-94
        bin counting, 87-94
        feature hashing, 84-87
chunking, 56
class-imbalanced dataset, 64
classification
    using k-means featurization, 122-127
    with logistic regression, 66-67
classification dataset, creating, 64
clustering algorithms, 116
    (see also k-means)

decomposition of, methods for, 189

matrix-vector formulation, principal components, 104

mean, 66

metric (k-means), 117

Microsoft Academic Graph dataset, 160

min-max scaling, 30
  caution when performing on sparse features, 32

missing data, 3

model evaluation, 3

model stacking, 6
  about, 128
  k-means featurization, 122-127
  key intuition for, 128

models
  about, 2
  based on space-partitioning trees, 6
  comparing, using hyperparameter tuning in, 68
  data scheme for academic paper recommender model, 162
  evaluating for use with categorical variable features, 95
  good linear model that is relatively unique, 191
  model-driven feature engineering, PCA as example of, 113

N

n-grams, 45, 52
  collocations vs., 53
  computing, 46

natural language processing (NLP), 52

neighborhoods (image), 142

neural networks (deep), learning image features with, 144-157
  convolutional layers, 146-150
  fully connected layers, 144
  pooling layers, 153
  ReLU transformation, 150-151
  response normalization layers, 151
  structure of AlexNet, 153-157

NLP (natural language processing), 52

NLTK Python package, 51

nonlinear dimensionality reduction, 115

nonlinear embedding, 116

nonlinear featurization, 115

nonlinear manifold feature extraction (k-means), 117

nonordinal values, 77

normalization, 5
  feature, 30
    (see also feature scaling)
  of gradient orientation histograms, 142
  response normalization layers in neural networks, 151

normalization constant, 33

null space, 188, 190

numeric data, 5-39
  counts, 8-15
    binarization, 9
    quantization or binning, 10-15
  feature scaling or normalization, 29-35
    min-max scaling, 30
    standardization (variance scaling), 31
    ℓ^2 normalization, 32
  feature selection, 38-39
  interaction features, 35-38
  log transformation, 15-29
    generalization of, in power transforms, 23-29
    using log transformed data to make predictions, 19-23
  scalars, vectors, and spaces, 6-8

NumPy sparse array, converting Pandas DataFrame to, 170

O

odds ratio for bin counting, 88

one-hot encoding, 78, 88
  of cluster membership categorical variable, 122
  dense featurization vs., 127
  pros and cons of, 83
  trade-offs, 94
  using scikit-learn DictVectorizer, 174
  vs. bin counting, 89

orthogonal basis, 185

orthogonal vectors, 184

orthogonality, 183

orthonormal basis, 183

P

Pandas
  computing quantiles and mapping data into quantile bins, 15

About the Authors

Alice Zheng is a technical leader in applied machine learning, spanning algorithm and platform development. Currently, she is a research science manager in Amazon Advertising. Previously, she worked on toolkit development and user education at GraphLab/Dato/Turi, and was a machine learning researcher at Microsoft Research. She holds a PhD in electrical engineering and computer science, and BA degrees in computer science and mathematics, all from UC Berkeley.

Amanda Casari is a leader and engineer who explores the next horizons of technology and how to best demonstrate the impacts these will bring. She is currently a senior product manager and data scientist in Concur Labs and cofounder of the Concur Labs AI Research team at SAP Concur. She has worked in a breadth of cross-functional roles and engineering disciplines for the last 16 years, including data science, machine learning, complex systems, and robotics. Amanda holds a BS in control systems engineering from the United States Naval Academy and an MS in electrical engineering from the University of Vermont.

Colophon

The animal on the cover of *Feature Engineering for Machine Learning* is a pharaoh eagle-owl (*Bubo ascalaphus*). This bird of prey is found in Northern Africa and the Arabian peninsula in rocky, arid habitat. It is among the smaller eagle-owls at 18–20 inches long, though the *Bubo* genus contains some of the largest owl species. Most eagle-owls (as well as their American cousins, horned owls) have distinctive ear tufts.

The pharaoh eagle-owl is nocturnal and hunts with a perching method. From a high vantage point, it waits for small mammals, snakes, lizards, birds, and even insects to come into range, before swiftly swooping toward its prey. It is well equipped for this with keen farsightedness and hearing, feathers optimized for silent flight, and sharp talons. Owls can also turn their heads in a range of about 270 degrees, allowing them to look behind themselves without making much movement.

This species has mottled brown, black, and white plumage, and distinctive orange-yellow eyes. Pharaoh owls are known to mate for life. Nesting sites are created in shallow scrapes among rocks, within crevices, or (occasionally) manmade structures like wells. In Egypt, the owls have been seen nesting on the pyramids.

Many of the animals on O'Reilly covers are endangered; all of them are important to the world. To learn more about how you can help, go to *animals.oreilly.com*.

The cover image is from *Elements of Ornithology*. The cover fonts are URW Typewriter and Guardian Sans. The text font is Adobe Minion Pro; the heading font is Adobe Myriad Condensed; and the code font is Dalton Maag's Ubuntu Mono.

Learn from experts.
Find the answers you need.

Sign up for a **10-day free trial** to get **unlimited access** to all of the content on Safari, including Learning Paths, interactive tutorials, and curated playlists that draw from thousands of ebooks and training videos on a wide range of topics, including data, design, DevOps, management, business—and much more.

Start your free trial at:
oreilly.com/safari

(No credit card required)